D0966591

LET'S GET FRANK

Let's Get Frank

CANADA'S MAD MAN OF ADVERTISING

Robin Brunet

Douglas &McIntyre

For Wendy:
Who knows you never get anywhere by being like everyone else.

DOUGLAS AND MCINTYRE (2013) LTD.
P.O. Box 219, Madeira Park, BC, V0N 2H0
www.douglas-mcintyre.com

Edited by Sara Weber
Text design by Shed Simas / Onça Design
Printed and bound in Canada
Printed on paper made from 100% post-consumer waste
Photos courtesy of Frank Palmer unless otherwise credited

Douglas and McIntyre (2013) Ltd. acknowledges the support of the Canada Council
for the Arts, which last year invested $153 million to bring the arts to Canadians
throughout the country. We also gratefully acknowledge financial support from
the Government of Canada and from the Province of British Columbia through the
BC Arts Council and the Book Publishing Tax Credit.

LIBRARY AND ARCHIVES CANADA CATALOGUING IN PUBLICATION
Brunet, Robin, author
    Let's get Frank : Canada's mad man of advertising / Robin Brunet.
Issued in print and electronic formats.
ISBN 978-1-77162-181-6 (hardcover).--ISBN 978-1-77162-182-3 (HTML)
    1. Palmer, Frank, 1940-. 2. Advertising executives--Canada--
Biography. 3. Businessmen--Canada--Biography. I. Title.
HF5810.P36B78 2018   659.1092   C2017-906343-X
                                              C2017-906344-8

Contents

CHAPTER ONE

Big Frankie P

Holding a large cappuccino, the unassuming client enters the reception area of a sleek downtown Vancouver office, where he notices a stuffed envelope on a nearby table. The unsealed envelope is labelled "Rattlesnake Eggs," and it belongs to the person he is supposed to meet: a tall, bald man with the build of an ex-prizefighter, who is standing beside the table.

"Rattlesnake eggs?" the client asks as they shake hands.

"Yeah. An idea I had for the food service industry."

"Food service? Like restaurants?"

The bald man sighs. "Don't laugh. Snake eggs are a delicacy in some countries. But not in Canada, unfortunately." The words are tinged with disappointment and disgust, discouraging conversation. So a silence ensues.

As the client sips his coffee, his eyes are fixed not on the bald man or the nearby receptionist, but on the envelope. How can eggs be so small as to fit into that? Probably dehydrated, he concludes. But if so, how can they possibly taste good?

After a long pause, the client asks, "Could I take a look? I've never seen rattlesnake eggs before."

The bald man shrugs. "If you want."

Still holding his cappuccino, the client picks up the envelope. It weighs almost nothing. He gently lifts the flap with one finger, and suddenly a sharp rattle pierces the air. He and his cappuccino jump backward.

After regaining his composure and dabbing coffee from his face and sweater, the client realizes the envelope contains a tightly wound rubber band attached to a noisemaker. He also notices the bald man looking directly at him, his eyes twinkling and a grin spreading over his face.

The gag is so corny that it's downright funny, and so too is the fact that this thuggish hulk of a man perpetrated it. The client starts laughing, and the bald man joins in. The receptionist politely looks away; she's witnessed her boss pull pranks like this plenty of times before, and she's more concerned right now that it's pouring rain outside, with a chance of snow.

The prankster and his victim are well aware of the lousy weather, but for a few dizzy moments it feels like summer to them.

*   *   *

The envelope's owner, Frank Palmer, is a legend in the Canadian advertising world. He not only developed Palmer Jarvis, one of the country's most acclaimed marketing communications agencies (and then became chairman and CEO of DDB Canada after selling Palmer Jarvis to the multinational advertising giant), but he is also credited with changing the face of Canadian advertising. "He's the only Western Canadian ad man who went to Toronto and wound up owning the town," says former employee and now friendly rival Chris Staples. "Previously, Vancouver was a graveyard for ad agencies. A million of them had come and gone over the decades."

One-time rival Bob Bryant, formerly of Bryant, Fulton & Shee Advertising Inc., elaborates: "What Frank also did that no other agency owner was able to do was become a star. No one else personified a company the way he did. He became the iconic brand of his own business."

In Canada, where those who rise to the top seem to do so almost apologetically, this is a rarity. DDB Canada president and chief operating officer Lance Saunders points out, "When I was hand-picked by Frank to help run DDB Canada in 2010, he had a celebrity quality: you instantly recognized him in a crowd and got nervous at the thought of approaching him. And he's achieved this degree of recognition because, unlike the vast majority of Canadian CEOs in any industry, he was never afraid to stick his head above the hole and take a position on issues."

The talent Palmer is most credited for is not his artistic skill (which is considerable) or a flair for writing (which Staples and many others say leaves a lot to be desired). "Instead, I think Frank's greatness—and uniqueness—is his ability to create an atmosphere in which great things happen," says Staples. "This is due to his almost childlike trust in people and his emotional openness. He's the last of the relationship guys."

Purely from a business standpoint, Palmer clawed his way to prominence, and his huge capacity for work remains undiminished. His ex-partner George Jarvis remarks, "When I first met Frank in the 1970s, I was dumbfounded by the number of jobs he could take on and accomplish well. Today, although I have long since opted for a different career and the role of a doting grandfather, Frank is still at it. He has out-worked, out-fought and out-competed everyone in the business, and now he's the last man standing in the ad world."

These qualities are matched by an enviable ability to foresee—and capitalize on—business and social trends. Saunders says, "The best of us have that ability to a degree, due to the voracious reading of trade journals, reports, a network of contacts and generally keeping our ears to the ground, but Frank's ability to predict what will be hot and what will not is extremely impressive."

Saunders adds, "Put it this way: he was the first to build an in-house social media department as well as a digital department, at a time when many experts thought these breakthroughs were just passing fancies. People thought he was nuts taking social media seriously, but look what happened. And today, we have fabulous big data and analytic groups in-house thanks to Frank's foresight.

"But instead of dwelling on these successes or going around saying 'I told you so,' his only interest is 'What's next?'"

Long-time friend and colleague Dean Mailey says Palmer "can't help but be embroiled in the future, no matter how tumultuous it may be: I too remember when social media emerged, and Frank, who was in his sixties, said to me, 'I'll make an extra million dollars by opening Tribal DDB,' which he described as a social media shop. I thought he was crazy." Today, the award-winning Tribal DDB specializes in interactive marketing; it conducts digital campaigns, produces online video and uses other cyber tools on behalf of clients such as Pepsi, Volkswagen, Nokia and Adidas.

Colleague Hugh Ruthven points out that Palmer's leadership style is unique. "He works well with senior management while staying very close and plugged in to the soldiers," he says. "He has always done this, having a good system for wiring himself in to the daily action and buzz of what's going on with clients and the business in general.

"He also has a pretty good nose for figuring out who the key influencers are, and then he stays close to them to obtain a constant read on what's going on at a day-to-day level. He has a lot of patience with smart people and very little for people he can't get creative thinking from. He tends to build a point of view about people quickly, which can be a strength and a weakness."

Ruthven, who is widely regarded as a master brand planner and who once worked as an account director and manager at DDB Canada, goes on to note that Palmer also has a reputation for being a meddler, calling it "a fault that we all clearly love him and hate him for. The intent on Frank's part is always to make things better. He wants to be in the centre of things, because that gives him purpose. This is his way of getting out of the ivory tower and making things happen."

To which Saunders adds, "By meddling, Frank will keep nudging people until they go in the right direction, and yes, this drives some people around the bend. But once they're on the path, he'll step back and offer his opinion only if asked for it. I have never once seen him interfere in the creative process."

Palmer is also an inspiration for people in other industries. Greg Klassen, a tourism industry strategist and a long-time client in his former capacity as CEO of the Canadian Tourism Commission, says, "While most advertising agency chiefs are struggling to retain advertising models of fifteen or twenty years ago, Frank is struggling to break free of all traditions and conventions. I often think of him as the Benjamin Button of the advertising world in that he seems to be aging in reverse, giving folk half his age a run for their money."

Palmer, seventy-eight in 2018, has been honoured, talked about in universities, interviewed by television talk show hosts, imitated, spoofed and revered. His rivals have also envied, criticized and gossiped about him—a sure measure of success.

As with many business leaders, Palmer is a study of contrasts. His penchant for playful gags is equalled only by his notorious reputation for obtaining clients at any cost. His considerable social charm conceals a personality that often craves solitude. On one hand he is almost recklessly devoted to helping friends in need; on the other, he will wait years to get even with people who he thinks have done him wrong.

An almost college student–like desire to "make a difference" governs many of Palmer's activities. "I don't want to do advertising for the sake of advertising, I want to do advertising that makes a difference," he told *Strategy* magazine. "I've always asked my staff to take some pride and give something back, and over the years we've put an awful lot back into things like the Kinsman Foundation of B.C., the Special Olympics, Ronald McDonald House Charities, Crime Stoppers—you name it. There are so many different needs out there."

More studies in contrast: whenever Vancouver's growing number of homeless approach Palmer for a handout, he unfailingly presses bills into their palms. On one occasion, a companion tells him, "He's just going to use the money to buy drugs—you know that, don't you?"

Palmer reacts as if he's personally offended. "He might also use it just to buy lunch; you know that too, don't you?"

Yet not a day goes by when Palmer doesn't make time to hurry over to a nearby hole-in-the-wall convenience store to buy a lottery ticket. If he doesn't have cash on hand, he'll borrow it from someone in the office, and upon obtaining the ticket he'll fold it carefully into his wallet, imagining the possibility of winning the jackpot. "Aren't you rich enough, Frank?" a friend asks, laughing, only to receive a cold stare tinged with fear in return. "I could be out on the street tomorrow. Wouldn't take much for that to happen."

Capping all of this is his uncanny knowledge of what constitutes effective advertising, and a business acumen that is encyclopedic. To paraphrase a famous ad slogan, "When Frank Palmer talks, people listen." After all, this is a man who generated $108 million in fees (not billings) in one year, which roughly translates into $800 million worth of sales.

Simply put, he has made a lot of money for a lot of people over the decades, and helped many companies earn a fortune.

Yet when his biographer first meets Palmer on a business matter in the winter of 2012, the first thing Palmer discusses, with undisguised glee, is the rattlesnake egg joke. He even produces the envelope that caused the cappuccino commotion just several days prior.

The discrepancy between his playfulness and his appearance is alarming. Dressed in a black suit and overcoat, Frank Palmer, with his bald head and thick neck, looks like someone you wouldn't want to encounter on a dark street. His gaze is vaguely threatening, and only the tendency of the corners of his mouth to turn upward suggests the humour within. Months later when his biographer tells him he initially thought Palmer looked like a thug, Palmer chuckles. "Not the first time I've heard that," he says. At least he no longer wears a goatee, which until recently caused strangers to suspect he was a Mafia don.

Young people are especially taken aback by Palmer's geniality. Recently, a British Columbia Institute of Technology student spent two months interning at DDB Canada, and at the end of her stint Palmer called her into his office and asked what she had learned. "I've learned that you're so easy to talk to," she gushed. Palmer smiles at the recollection: "At least that was an improvement over what she said when she first met me. She said, 'I'm in awe of you!'"

Several weeks after Palmer describes his rattlesnake egg gag, his biographer visits the downtown Vancouver headquarters of DDB Canada, of which Palmer is chairman and CEO. It may not be the biggest ad agency in terms of physical size, but the reception area is modern, sleek and spotless. The finishes and lighting are high-end, and Kirsty, the young woman behind the tall counter, greets visitors with a dazzling smile.

Unfortunately, on the day of the biographer's visit, Kirsty is frowning at the flat-screen TV mounted on the wall beside her. It's supposed to be fixed to a single channel, but—maybe because of the heavy rain outside—the channel keeps changing. Kirsty aims a remote at the flat screen and clicks to the correct channel, but it changes again.

By the time Palmer materializes (he has an unnerving habit of doing so; even on concrete flooring his footsteps are silent), Kirsty is clicking at the television like a movie cop firing bullets at a felon. "What in hell's going on here?" he asks.

"I'm sorry, but this TV . . ." Kirsty stifles an expletive, and to her further aggravation the channels start flipping like the pages of a book.

Palmer turns to his biographer and produces a key fob from his pocket. "You see, this device can manipulate flat screens from a distance, as long as you aim it at the television . . ."

Palmer's pranks are as famous as his ad campaigns, and he enjoys recounting them almost as much as he does perpetrating them. The one he loves telling the most is the time he snuck into colleague Bob Stamnes's bathroom while Stamnes was taking a shower (after a particularly heavy night of drinking) and carefully emptied a glass of red wine between Stamnes's legs, causing Stamnes to leap in horror at the blood-coloured liquid when he looked down.

One reason colleagues such as Stamnes took the gags in stride is because they were matched just as frequently by friendly overtures, such as the time when Stamnes turned forty and Palmer hired a limousine to escort Stamnes and his girlfriend to a local restaurant. As a staunch supporter of the Vancouver Police drill team, Palmer also persuaded four motorcycle cops to give them an escort, sirens sounding, through Vancouver's downtown core.

To some degree, the pranks and the grandiose stunts were part and parcel of what Palmer frequently refers to "as the fun days of advertising," and just like the antics of early-twentieth-century news reporters, they buffered what was a demanding, often cutthroat profession.

The ad game is just as cutthroat today, but the jokes, along with the heroic capacity for self-abuse many of its players exercised, have largely been replaced by cheerless corporate codes of conduct. Many old-timers say more's the pity; what ad man of today will, when he reaches his seventies, double over with laughter at the memory of a well-staged prank or think wistfully of illicit liaisons that shouldn't have happened but did? Or, for that matter, be motivated to still arrive at work at seven every morning, as Palmer does routinely?

For every memorable ad campaign, Palmer can recall a prank or funny encounter. "It's the laughter that kept us going and enabled us to fulfill all kinds of outlandish demands and deadlines," he explains.

In short, it kept them young—or at least energized. "I'm constantly urging newcomers to this business to have fun with what they do," says the man who once placed a dead octopus under a colleague's pillow during a fishing trip. "But too often the message goes over their heads."

*　　*　　*

Of the many factors that influenced Palmer as a kid growing up in Vancouver's Kitsilano neighbourhood, three are especially noteworthy. "Mom used to hide in closets and jump out when I entered the room," he recalls with a grin. "She used to balance pots and pans over the front door when she knew Russell, my dad, was going to try to sneak home late. She was always game for a good joke."

The second influence was his mother Phyllis's habit of snatching Russell's paycheque from his hand when he arrived home with it every week, and giving him an allowance instead. "That used to drive me crazy," Palmer says. "To me, the sight of a grown man having his hard-earned money managed by someone else was embarrassing and deeply humiliating, and early on I vowed that if anyone was going to dole out allowances when I became an adult, it would be me."

Even though Palmer discovered much later in life that Phyllis grabbed the paycheques to curb Russell's pub crawls and gambling, to this day Palmer turns pale at the thought of being dependent on someone else for money. As a rich man, he loves nothing better than formulating ways of generating funds for worthy causes.

"It's safe to say that Frank has always been obsessed with money," says lifelong friend Brian Robertson. "Not so much in terms of personal wealth; he learned long ago how to make money for himself, so that's no big deal. Instead, he's obsessed with making money for other people such as his DDB colleagues and clients. He'll go out of his way to concoct schemes for making money for charity. He loves nothing better than to open his chequebook for a worthy cause, and that generosity of spirit was evident when he and I were teenagers attending Kitsilano High School."

Hugh Ruthven offers another perspective on Palmer's relationship with money. In 2008, when writing an internal document about the ten reasons for Palmer's success, Ruthven listed "Frank the Financier" as the sixth reason: "Frank loves money only because it buys freedom, a bit of 'I told you so, so fuck off' . . . Frank loves to make bonuses because they gauge success."

A third childhood influence contributed to Palmer's adult mindset and made him a great—instead of merely a good—ad man. "I'll never forget being a boy of about seven, standing with classmates waiting to be picked for a baseball team," he recalls. "To my humiliation I was picked dead last, and I remember thinking at the time that when I got older I would make damned sure to be a picker instead of someone waiting to be snapped up."

Indeed, by the time Palmer was in his late teens he was six foot one and weighed a muscular 210 pounds (courtesy of weight-lifting), perfect for football. "My peers kept insisting I join the team, but I had no interest. The more people tried to get me to do things, the more I resisted. I had my own pursuits and ideas about how to live life, and I stuck by them." Subsequently, Palmer had his own ideas about what made good advertising and how to grow a company—and he stuck by them.

But even more profoundly, the humiliation at being picked last gave Palmer a sense of competitiveness (some would say a taste for revenge) that has enraged rivals and bothered even close friends. "There's nothing subtle about Frank," says George Jarvis. "He will do absolutely anything to get to the next step. This has served him extremely well in the ad game and perhaps even in some aspects of his personal life, but it's not without drawbacks. I for one was worn down by it, and it's worn down other people close to him."

Bob Bryant remarks, "When I was in the ad business, Frank wasn't just a rival, he was the enemy. For example, all of the agencies in town had a gentlemen's agreement not to steal accounts from one another, but such rules never applied to Frank. A lot of ad men were pissed off when they took clients to lunch, only to discover they had been approached by Frank."

Palmer's former executive assistant of nearly twenty years, Hilary Robertson, grew to know Palmer to the point where "if we got into an argument, we would shout things at one another that shocked onlookers, and yet we didn't think anything of it."

That said, she's at a loss to explain Palmer's roller-coaster personality. "On one hand he was incredibly generous and protective, especially of me, yet he also had a mean streak and could be incredibly insensitive. He thought nothing of exploiting people's weaknesses."

So why does Robertson value Palmer's friendship to this day? "He was so charismatic and such a fascinating study of contrasts that I couldn't help but like him from the beginning," she replies. "I thought his private life was a mess, especially with the women earlier in his life. But contrasting that was the fact he took his role as an employer very seriously. And he always got what he wanted, which in a strange way is also attractive.

"I often think of him as a big spider, constantly spinning his web and sitting in the middle of it patiently, sure in the knowledge that the people he needs or wants will eventually be caught."

To many professional women, Palmer, in all his manly, flawed glory, is an irresistible package. "I adore him," says Sue Belisle, president and publisher of *Business in Vancouver*, one-time board member of NABS West, and chair of the society's annual golf tournament. "We've been close friends for years, so I've heard all the drinking and women stories of his past, and he wouldn't be Frank without them. It's rare these days to find someone who always speaks his mind and never bullshits. And those people who truly call him a friend know he has a heart of gold."

Sharing the maelstrom that tends to be Palmer's daily life is his wife of twenty-four years, Marika. More than anyone, Marika has been exposed to all the facets of his personality, and guards secrets that are for her eyes and ears only. A flamboyant character in her own right, Marika has no problem bluntly expressing her opinion of people, and she has a knack for doing so in public settings.

Although Palmer has caused Marika a fair share of headaches, she confesses to an acquaintance one morning, "I'm more in love with him than ever. He's a tough man in a tough business, but the real Frank Palmer actually hates confrontation. Many of his so-called friends and partners have sensed that and taken advantage of him over the years, and I've done my best to remove them from the picture."

When asked to clarify, Marika takes a long drag from a newly lit cigarette and exhales. "Sorry, wrong choice of words. I should have said 'gotten rid of them.'" If Palmer has a rival for stubbornness and unpredictability, it comes in the form of a five-foot-four-inch woman who welcomes him home every night.

Alan Gee, who co-founded the advertising firm Blammo Worldwide in Toronto (which in 2016 merged with Extreme Group to form Arrivals+Departures), thinks one of Palmer's greatest assets is his ability to make everyone he comes in contact with think they're his friend. "I suppose it's because he's so honest, but even casual acquaintances come away after a brief meeting assuming he's a confidante. They regard Frank as a cool guy they want to hang out with, and I suspect Frank realized this at an early age and has been exploiting it ever since. It's how he's able to get the inside scoop on anything he wants."

Palmer is candid about his ferocious drive, and during one conversation with his biographer, the reason for it is boiled down to its essence. "Frank, why are you so competitive?"

"Because I want to win," he replies.

"Why?"

"Because winning means success."

"But what does success give you?"

"It gives me control."

"And what does control give you?"

"It lets me chart my own course in life."

Palmer reclines in his chair and puts his fingertips together to form a steeple. His gaze is steady. You can do a lot to Frank, but don't meddle with his hold over his own destiny.

*   *   *

Palmer loves telling people that DDB Canada is the most awarded agency in the history of advertising on the Canadian scene. It's a shameless boast, but that of a proud father. As far back as 1999 he was telling reporters that his daily role at his agency was one of "chief cheerleader. I don't have the pompoms, but I'm there cheering for the team, giving high fives and celebrating wins. And I'm trying to encourage personal development. I want to give people the opportunity to grow."

The late 1990s were a major turning point for Palmer and his agency. In November 1997 he sold Palmer Jarvis Communications—the business he built from the ground up with much sweat, heartache and risk taking that would have driven lesser men to nervous collapse—to DDB Worldwide Communications Group Inc., a division of Omnicom Group Inc. based in New York City. Palmer Jarvis merged with the Toronto subsidiary of DDB Needham Worldwide and became Palmer Jarvis DDB (later rebranded as DDB Canada).

Overnight Palmer's business transformed from a highly regarded Western Canadian agency to one that was able to service international accounts. "To be in the game today you really have to be international," he told the press following the merger. "You can't afford to stay the same size. So would I do it again? In a New York second."

Although he had been courted by numerous multinational agencies, he found DDB's culture the only one that was compatible with his own: "When I met with the principals, I was impressed with how they treated me. I had talked to other groups over the years about doing partnerships, but when it came down to it they treated me like a zero—and part of this was due to me being based in Western Canada, which was regarded as small potatoes and inconsequential to the bigger picture. The DDB people, on the other hand, made me feel that I was of value. And they've never deviated."

Keith Bremer, the chief financial officer of DDB Worldwide, who is based in New York, recalls meeting Palmer when the sale was taking place. "Apart from the fact he was very personable and engaging, which is what you need to be in this industry in order to attract clients, I was impressed by his business acumen right off the bat, and soon I appreciated the great insight he had about what clients want.

"As for him having developed all of this in Western Canada, it neither surprised us, nor could we have cared less. Talent is talent. We got him to lead Canada for us, and he's one of our best executives."

Palmer's praise of DDB notwithstanding, his sale of Palmer Jarvis surprised many who knew him as a person who enjoyed total control over every aspect of business. Palmer, the maverick ad man of the 1970s and '80s, acquiescing to higher powers in the corporate world? Answering to shareholders rather than his own gut? It didn't seem likely.

Indeed, twenty years after the dust had settled, when he is asked to summarize his feelings about the sale, he chooses his words carefully. "It was the best thing I ever did and it was also the worst thing I ever did," he replies. And that is that.

Vancouver broadcast veteran Red Robinson implicitly understands Palmer's cryptic comment. "Frank sold to DDB because he was looking after his staff and wanted to make sure they had long and fruitful careers," he says. "I don't think he did it because he wanted to on a personal level."

Chris Staples, who was working for Palmer as national creative director during the buyout, has a contrary opinion. "He sold the company to gain respect and get a lot of money, and I say good for him—although at the time it angered a lot of colleagues, including me. The trouble was, although the sale made him rich, answering to shareholders instead of his gut became a major bone of contention."

In 1997 Palmer Jarvis DDB collected so many trophies at the Marketing Awards in Toronto that Staples's table collapsed under the weight, causing champagne glasses, cutlery and plates to crash to the ground. At the British Columbia Lotus Awards that same year, the agency was nominated for so many honours that the ceremony's hosts arranged for a chair onstage especially for Staples, so he wouldn't have to keep walking to the podium.

Two years later Palmer Jarvis DDB won a Gold Lion, one of the top prizes at the Cannes Lions International Festival of Creativity in France, and the first one in the television category for Canada since 1981.

Of the avalanche of accolades DDB Canada (as it's known today) has collected since then, Palmer notes, "It has been said we've won more awards in Canada than any agency, times two."

During the early weeks of this book project, Palmer repeats the same remark. Like the laughter provoked by his gags, awards mean a lot to him. On a personal level, they reaffirm his worth. Professionally, they are crucial to DDB Canada's reputation. "Competitors are always breathing down your neck in this business," he explains. "Awards are one indication that you've still got the jump on them."

But even deeper than on a personal level, winning is an instinctual need for Palmer, something embedded in the reptilian part of his brain. And now, in an era when progressive teaching dictates that all school kids should receive awards merely for participating in events, Palmer takes every opportunity to discuss the value of winning to younger folk.

One venue in which he has a captive audience is *Frankly Speaking*, an online column he writes weekly for DDB Canada staff. In a summer 2013 column he poses the question, Is winning a Cannes Lion important?

If you do a quick search online for winning quotes, hundreds will pop up. One of the best-known quotes is from American football coach Vince Lombardi: "Winning isn't everything; it's the only thing . . .

I don't know about you, but winning for me is very important. It's connected to almost everything we do in business, and the people we look up are usually those who are successful in life. Winning is also important to our clients who want to be the best in their business category, in order to keep ahead of their competition.

In our early years at school, we were all taught to be competitive. I remember sack races, relay races, tug-a-wars, shot put, high jump and other competitions that tested our strength and agility. Those who placed first, second and third were awarded colourful little ribbons. We raced home to show these ribbons and good report cards to our parents and hoped we'd made them proud. And when we didn't win, we felt like losers.

I believe we're all born to win and be competitive, because it's all about aspirations and pursuing our goals and ambitions. No one gets out of bed and starts their day saying, "Today I'm going to fail . . ."

In our business, winning is also all about scoring. Over the past seventeen years, DDB Canada has dominated *Strategy*'s Creative Report Card, which ranks the country's top agencies, clients and creative talent based on award show honours. Our long, rich history of winning has earned the agency almost double the number of points than the next runner up on the report card. Our most recent wins at Cannes are equivalent to winning an Oscar or an Olympic Gold Medal. It proves our ideas are amongst the best in the world. So the answer is yes, winning a Cannes Lion is important.

I believe winning is what sets us apart and drives us to be more passionate, productive, and purposeful and to have a prosperous life. It confirms that we are the best in what we do.

* * *

If celebrity has become an inextricable component of Palmer's career at this stage of the game, he uses it more often than not to poke fun at himself.

For example, to publicize the 2012 NABS Vintage Auction (which he engineered), a video was produced in which a young man emerges from a washroom stall to find Palmer rinsing his hands at the sink. "Frank? Frank Palmer?"

"Yeah."

Dumbfounded, the youth blurts, "It's an honour to meet you! I can't believe this—you're an advertising legend. I'm a huge admirer of your work. You founded Palmer Jarvis in '69, merged with DDB, got named Canadian Agency of the Year for, what, nine years in a row, DDB Canada's been named one of the top agencies on the planet by the *Gunn Report* . . ."

Bewildered, Palmer asks, "Who are you?"

"I'm an art director," the youth replies. "A junior art director. Anyways, I heard that you're going to be interning with us today for NABS."

"Well, it's a good cause."

Suddenly emboldened, the youth pulls five dollars from his pocket and gives it to Palmer. "Yeah. Well, you know what, intern? You can go grab me a coffee."

Standing with the bill in his hand, Palmer asks incredulously, "Are you kidding?"

As he turns to leave, the youth replies, "Decaf—bitch." The video ends with the message, "Make a top dog your bitch."

Palmer wasn't finished making fun of himself for that event. Decked out in gangsta chains, short pants and mod sunglasses with a cap on backward, he graced the front cover and back page of the November 2012 edition of *Strategy* magazine. The premise was that although he was willing to auction his services off for charity, he wanted to remind the industry "that there's no intern quite as badass as Big Frankie P," as he was quoted in the issue.

The outrageous sight of Big Frankie P was accompanied by spectacularly awful rap lyrics: "Aw hell yeah I'm the cream of the crop/Writin' website copy, rising straight to the top/Never had an intern like Big Frankie P/Gonna win your agency a Coupon Grand Prix."

There's no question Palmer enjoys the limelight; after all, the bigger the audience, the more chances he gets to play practical jokes and tell funny stories. However, the cumulative message of his amusing videos, television appearances, campy magazine covers and entertaining speeches is familiar: "Loosen up. You have to work hard in the ad game, and it takes its toll on you unless you're careful."

That message prompted him, after decades of aborted attempts, to finally hire someone to commit his story to paper. On one especially cheery spring morning in his office, as he looks down on the BC Supreme Court complex, he rubs a hand over his scalp and declares, "I've never taken myself seriously, and I can't stand ego clashes. This industry is full of them, but thank goodness I created a company and retained talent that had no time for such nonsense."

True to his habit of jumping from one train of thought to another he says, "As George Jarvis and others have noted, I'm probably the oldest guy left in this business operating at this level, and people are asking me to do more, not less. Which suits me just fine, because although the industry is less fun overall, I'm having a ball—and hopefully everyone else in this office is too."

Pausing for a second, he concludes, "I realize I have more of a past than I do a future. If I were a golfer, I would say that I'm on the eighteenth hole. But if I had to die tomorrow, I would do so knowing I've had a pretty good time.

"The thing is, I don't want to die tomorrow. I plan to be like George Burns and live to one hundred. And during that time, if I can convince younger folk not to take things so seriously so that they can keep working hard over the long haul, then all the better."

Such a comment is hardly surprising to Hugh Ruthven: "Frank's a guy who never expected to get to the level of business success he's at, and maintaining that success is what drives him every day. Does he really have to worry about success anymore? Of course not—but what about the others? Will they constantly evolve or become stale and predictable? Frank worries mostly about that."

Analyze This

Ad men have been called manipulators, hucksters, propagandists, snake-oil salesmen and worse. One reason for the animosity toward them (an animosity some say is generally harboured by highbrow types employed in the halls of academe) is that the canvas they use to develop their campaigns is literally anything: all forms of traditional and electronic mass media, buses, park benches, buildings—even humans and the sky itself (in the form of that quaint and wonderful skill, skywriting). You can't get away from advertising no matter how hard you try, and by extension you can't get away from ad men.

The animosity is also fuelled by the perception that ad men are responsible for consumerism run rampant. At best, critics will define advertising as a form of communication used to persuade or manipulate an audience to take some form of action.

Humber College, in its History of Creative Advertising course, offers this description of the industry: "Advertising is a part of modern culture. As an effective discourse, advertising signifies certain ideals and values, shaping and changing the way we perceive and understand the social world. The real and sometimes surreal effects of advertising challenge the way we identify our social environments including the family, work, and even international relations."

Descriptions such as the above invariably make the corners of Palmer's mouth turn upward. "And here I am, having spent all those decades just making sure we delivered memorable campaigns on deadline," he says.

Arguably, ad men are treated with a little more respect in Europe—at least by the media. In October 2012, Sir Martin Sorrell, head of the world's largest advertising network (WPP), made headlines when he announced that product demand had ground to a halt. He became the focus of serious debate after claiming that problems in the eurozone, volatility in the Middle East, the slowdown in the Chinese economy and the US fiscal deficit were four "shocks" that could disrupt the world economy within the year.

Normally such predictions are given credence only when economists utter them, but as the British news website *The Independent* pointed out on October 26, 2012, "Advertising is the classic lead indicator. It tells you precisely, maybe brutally, what businesses think about future demand—for you don't advertise unless you think that ad spend will be rewarded by demand for the product."

That's a far cry from North American deep thinkers dismissing advertising as the practice of persuading people to buy things they don't need—a charge Palmer has learned to laugh off.

But in a consumer-driven society, the ad man's image as a commodities peddler is perhaps indelible, fortified by popular television programs like *Mad Men*, which painted the industry in the 1960s as populated by amoral, philandering sharks. Incidentally, although Palmer's business dealings have always been guided by a strong sense of right and wrong, he nonetheless has fond regard for that defunct program. "The first season was pretty accurate in terms of the way business was conducted back then," he says. "We all drank and smoked heavily and played around. But we were way less serious than the characters in that show. We had a good time. And we did some damned good work."

For those who maintain the view that ad men primarily peddle consumer goods, the question must be asked, What came first: the product or the ad campaign? Many professors inform their students that advertising came along during the era of industrialization about 150 years ago, and that it kindled public desire for commodities that would make people's lives easier (as if the great unwashed, saddled as they were with horrendous physical and social burdens, didn't yearn for an easier life all by themselves).

Commodities may be the most obvious focus for ad agencies, but something far more primordial drives ad men: the deeply human urge to promote human activity in all its glory, whether it's an event, a social cause or the manufacture of a new car.

In this regard, advertising is inextricably linked to journalism and dates as far back as ancient Egypt, when papyrus was used to make sales messages and posters. Archaeology has proven that billboards are the oldest form of advertising (it's no coincidence that advertising quickly became a visual medium during the Middle Ages, due to a populace that was illiterate).

The modern advertising industry that would propel Palmer and many others to fame had its roots in eighteenth-century British newspapers, which ran ads for goods and services; in Canada, the industry began in 1752 according to the *Canadian Encyclopedia*, with an offer of butter for sale in a government publication called the *Halifax Gazette*; in 1764 the *Québec Gazette* (later renamed the *Chronicle-Telegraph*) was founded and reportedly carried as much news about merchandise as it did events.

Advertising in Canada blossomed in the nineteenth century. In June 1836, the Montreal newspaper *La Presse* was the first publication in the country to include paid advertising in its pages, which in turn allowed the owners to lower its price, extend its readership and increase its profitability. Newspapers across the nation soon copied the formula.

By 1889 newspapers had become so replete with advertising that thirty-four-year-old journalist Anson McKim decided to open an office in Montreal to arrange the placement of advertisements in Ontario newspapers. His reasoning was simple: if he could place the same advertisement in a large number of Canadian dailies, the economic impact would be exponential.

McKim's business, A. McKim and Company, was Canada's first advertising agency, and it is credited with developing a newspaper directory that listed periodicals by province, city and village along with information about these places—an essential tool in understanding the markets connected with individual newspapers.

McKim is also credited with establishing the way advertising agencies are paid: he received commissions from the newspapers that featured advertisements prepared by his agency. To this day, commissions paid by the advertisers remain the principal source of ad agency income.

By 1900, forty years before Palmer was born, advertisers hoping to influence Canada's five million inhabitants could choose from 112 daily newspapers serving 570,000 subscribers (according to the *Canadian Encyclopedia*); general-interest magazines; special-interest magazines; and street posters, which delivered inexpensive and graphic messages. Mail-order catalogues from retailers helped foster a national market because their advertisements for merchandise reached millions of farm and town people.

Flash forward to the current millennium: in 2015, the global media agency Carat estimated that annual spending on advertising had grown to $529 billion internationally, with digital media being the prime venue in which ads appeared.

*   *   *

As with so much of Canada's heritage, the history of advertising north of the forty-ninth parallel is sketchy because few agencies have bothered to maintain solid records. "It's a tragedy, considering the huge degree advertising has influenced society," says Bob Stamnes, owner and president of Elevator Strategy, Advertising & Design (now abbreviated to Elevator), which is based in Vancouver. "The enormous and dazzling output of the McKims, the Cockfield Browns, the Baker Lovicks and so many other creative forces in this country are just a memory."

Ad men such as Stamnes, who turned fifty-eight in 2017, are the last link to the classic industry players whose carousing, double-crossing and sheer gusto for the work are in sharp contrast to the muted pastels of twenty-first-century business conduct. "It was my privilege to become friends with one of the last great ad men, Jerry Goodis, when he was working at the University of Victoria and I was a student," says Stamnes, whose animated way of talking complements his penchant for dressing in florid bow ties with colours matching his glasses, shirts and shoes.

Goodis, based in Ontario, was among many other things responsible for Canadian catchphrases such as "We care about the shape you're in" (Wonderbra), "At Speedy you're a somebody" (Speedy Muffler King) and "Harvey's makes your hamburger a beautiful thing" (Harvey's). "He was also a top advisor for nineteen years to Pierre Trudeau, and he used to tell great stories about sneaking the former prime minister through the back doors so he could hook up with Barbra Streisand," says Stamnes. "People like Goodis and Palmer were genuine mentors to me. More importantly, they changed Canada, and unless museums and other institutions decide to dedicate permanent space to the world of advertising, even the memories of what they created will vanish."

Stamnes is asked by a friend intent on playing devil's advocate, "So, what if it all gets lost in time?"

Stamnes patiently replies, "Then it'll be a tragedy for the ad industry. Because all the great stories, not to mention the ad campaigns themselves, gave younger people like me a zeal for the profession. And the zeal inspired great work."

Some Canadians have sought to preserve the remnants. Brock University professor Russell Johnston used existing archival sources and data from trade magazines to trace the industry's development from the late nineteenth century to the 1930s; the result was *Selling Themselves: The Emergence of Canadian Advertising* (University of Toronto Press, 2001).

In *Selling Themselves*, Johnston explains how the evolution of Canadian cities, technological advances in printing and a surge in the availability of consumer products transformed newspapers from partisan journals to commercial publications with advertising space to fill. This was the ideal breeding ground for the modern advertising agent, who could assure businesses that whatever messages they wanted to spread would reach the right audience.

Johnston also describes how ad men in Toronto negotiated with media organizations to develop standards, including agency agreements, standardization of commission rates and rate cards, audited circulations, and business practice improvements.

Additionally, Johnston chronicles how by the 1930s psychological methods, research and planning were being used in marketing strategies: "No longer would managers have to base crucial decisions on their impressions and guesswork concerning the market for their goods."

The online Canadian Advertising Museum picks up where Johnston leaves off. It notes that the ad industry blossomed when World War II troops returned home and bought houses, furniture and appliances, with their top priority being cars. The museum notes, "Sixty-one radio stations opened between 1945 and 1952. Advertising took advantage of radio's growth by filling the airwaves with jingles selling everything from toothpaste to the week's grocery deals."

While the modern wave of ad men honed their skills during the 1940s, Frank Palmer was spending as much free time as he could at the beach, which was a short walk from his Kitsilano family home. "As for school, I hated it," he says. "That's partly because at the age of eight I began making money at a variety of jobs: paper boy, meat delivery boy, helping my dad at the bakery he worked in. Making money struck me as a far more attractive pursuit."

Palmer's childhood knowledge of advertising was limited to enjoying billboard and print ads; when he wasn't making money or hanging out at the beach, he was developing a talent for sketching.

It's worth noting that most North American ad agencies in the first half of the twentieth century weren't big. They had largely grown from a single person or a partnership such as Batten, Barton, Durstine & Osborn, a.k.a. BBDO. But they were populated by a seemingly endless array of creative geniuses who turned the small agencies into huge ones: characters such as Raymond Rubicam, who with John Orr Young created the Young & Rubicam agency in New York in 1923, widely considered a model for the industry. Young & Rubicam was the first agency to use scientific telephone sampling and test audiences to measure the success of commercials and advertisements.

Another creative genius (and one who Palmer greatly admires) was David Ogilvy. Born in the UK, Ogilvy was a former chef, researcher and farmer who launched Hewitt, Ogilvy, Benson & Mather in New York in the 1940s. He was famous for countless unforgettable ad campaigns, among them the catchphrase "At sixty miles an hour, the loudest noise in this new Rolls-Royce comes from the electric clock." He was also responsible for the immortal slogan "Only Dove is one-quarter moisturizing cream." Ogilvy was fond of telling clients, "The consumer is not a moron. She's your wife!"

Yet another master was Leo Burnett, who joined the fold in the 1930s and went on to create Leo Burnett Company, based in Chicago. It became one of only a handful of top ten US agencies not headquartered in New York City (decades later, the company would employ Lance Saunders, born in Montreal and raised in Toronto, who today helps oversee DDB Canada in conjunction with Palmer).

By the end of the 1950s Leo Burnett was billing $100 million annually. One of Burnett's habits was to compile a compendium of words, phrases and analogies that struck him as being particularly apt in expressing an idea. His philosophy—"When you reach for the stars, you may not quite get one, but you won't come up with a handful of mud either"—enabled him to create classic ad campaigns and characters, including the Jolly Green Giant.

The Canadian Advertising Museum describes the ad industry in the 1950s as follows: "The first two TV stations in 1952 (CBFT in Montreal and CBLT in Toronto) reached 10 per cent of the people. By 1959, forty-eight stations were reaching 75 per cent. Advertising revenues on television rose by 1,400 per cent in just seven years."

As for the 1960s—a decade that young adult Palmer casting about for a career kicked off by attempting to join the Vancouver Police Department—the museum notes that advertising echoed the experimentation going on in the outside world and "focused on creating concepts, the big idea. We broke the rules and experimented with everything. And advertising reflected it all."

By the end of the 1960s Palmer was a bona fide ad man, and he agrees with the museum's assessment of that decade: "It was the first time that less was valued as more: fewer words, more impact," he says. "That was a revolutionary concept, and it inspired me."

The Canadian Advertising Museum characterizes the 1970s as a time when "the wild creativity of the '60s left clients wondering if it really swayed opinions and sold product. Everything had to be researched to be sure. It was an era that brought in 'positioning,' where your product was positioned against the competition. Film was beginning to be replaced by video and nearly all commercials were in colour. Thirty-second commercials were more popular than sixty. It was an omen for the future. Life was becoming faster."

According to the museum, the 1980s were all about "boldness," and the 1990s were when technology truly revolutionized the advertising world in the form of the world wide web, which debuted in 1992: "Four years into the decade, 3 million people were online, and another four years later another 100 million were emailing, shopping at e-stores and running their businesses on e-commerce."

For his part, Palmer is as comfortable with the cyber world as any attention-challenged youth, but he still types with his two middle fingers—a sure sign of an old-world ad man (or journalist). He responds to more texts during the course of a day than an ardent, love-struck teen, but at the same time he tinkers with the idea of leading a national campaign to abolish cell phone use for one day a year, just to give younger folk a taste of what silence used to sound like.

He also reserves a special contempt for the large-screen Apple computer on his desk. "I'd put a bullet through this fucking thing if I could," he mutters every time he uses the keyboard.

Palmer is the classic 1960s ad man still flourishing in a technology-obsessed world where people spend most of their waking moments staring at screens, immersed in sound and fury. His habit of telling stories about famous ad campaigns or the wild cast of characters he knew decades ago isn't because he's living in the past. It's because the stories are more relevant than ever.

Many of the stories contain old-fashioned values (even though their intention is merely to entertain), and others simply serve to show how much fun life used to be when it was lived large. "It's funny how you remember one person in your past, and that leads to other memories being unlocked and other characters you've forgotten," Palmer says during an informal get-together. "The ad game was a great place to meet characters; I learned a lot from them."

And at a time in history when social media is reinventing industries such as advertising and journalism, Palmer is more determined than ever to dig in his heels and emphasize values from his era that millennials too often skim over. "Millennials are far smarter and in some ways better than the best of my generation ever was, but a lot of them are too undisciplined for their own good," he says. "Part of this stems from being in a world where everything is instant, no waiting. In other words, you're caught up in this crazy velocity of disseminating information, and the sheer speed causes you to overlook details. The trouble is, details are essential to business. Always have been, always will be, regardless of how much technology changes our lives."

Palmer leans forward in his chair. "I always remember this story about the Bank of British Columbia, which was a client of ours for seventeen years before HSBC took it over. We were in the bank's boardroom with the president at the time, and the printer came in and delivered some business cards. The president—new to the job—was quite excited and took out a card, and it was so flimsy it curled over."

Palmer smiles. "The president said, pointing at the card and referring to the printer, 'I don't know who they are, but obviously they don't know who I am. Get rid of them.'

"We weren't the printer, thank goodness. But what he was saying, obviously, was that if they can't take care of the little details, they can't take care of my annual report."

Here's positive news for us "older" folk, just in case any of you are getting the gears from some of the younger staff (and by older, I mean fifty-plus).

Many stereotypes about older workers simply aren't true. For example, it's been said that they can't or won't learn new skills. But in reality, those over fifty are proving their ability to learn new skills by being the fastest-growing group of internet users. Bet you didn't know that! Proof that we're in the digital age, not the Stone Age.

Another interesting fact is workers between forty-five and fifty-five stay with an organization twice as long as those between twenty-five and thirty-five—and they take fewer sick days.

These facts are important, as there's a looming workforce shortage. But I know that we fifty-plus folk are sometimes challenged when looking for a different job or career. The advertising business is and has always been considered a youth-centric occupation (you might not have guessed that if you've been watching *Mad Men*).

Jobs in communications, marketing, entertainment etc. all seem to have an age limit, but there are many advantages that we "fine-wine" types can offer. If you are fifty-plus there's still lots of life in you and opportunities ahead. As for all you younger employees, there's still hope for you: you'll get to be fifty-plus at some point too.

—FRANK PALMER

An Hour with Palmer

T o outsiders, Palmer is a serious individual, not to be crossed, not the sort of person to try to engage in meaningless chit-chat. In a room full of strangers he sizes up each person. In business meetings he listens intently to what everyone has to say and then, more often than not, he either dominates the conversation or makes a few laser-sharp observations that qualify him as leader of the pack. As a seasoned ad man he exhibits all the hallmarks of a consummate professional, right down to his terse but pointed replies to incoming email.

But Palmer also yearns to know the people around him. Meet him more than once, and he'll start asking questions. Once it's established that you have a talent or passion, or are merely embroiled in something interesting, he will begin to let his guard down.

You don't have to cross Palmer's path too often before he starts telling stories. He has very few acquaintances, only strangers and friends, and over the decades his friends have grown accustomed to his habit of jumping abruptly from one topic of conversation to the next. He'll also routinely interrupt someone else's train of thought with a comment that has little if anything to do with the matter at hand.

Are these ad-man tactics or are they Palmer's way of getting the most out of a discussion? "I like mixing things up and keeping things a little off balance," is all he will admit to. "Keeping people on their toes, me included, has certain benefits."

Palmer's penchant for switching discussion topics—sometimes in mid-sentence—is entirely in keeping with other personality dichotomies. Anyone who has spent time with him will attest that his passion for business deals and numbers is matched only by his love for mysticism. A guest learns this early on, when during a heated conversation about workplace liability, Palmer suddenly asks, "What sign are you?"

"What do you mean, 'sign'?"

"Your astrological sign; what is it?"

"I have no idea, Frank."

Palmer's mouth falls open in genuine shock. "What the fuck do you mean, you don't know? Everybody knows their sign. What's wrong with you?"

Incensed, Palmer jumps out of his chair and stalks out of his office, muttering, "Fucking guy doesn't even know his own sign." He returns a few minutes later, clutching a newspaper and sits beside the guest, grinning. "The papers print your horoscope every day, so no matter where you are, all you need to do is open to the correct page to find out what your day will be like."

The matter of workplace liability completely abandoned, Palmer opens the newspaper to the horoscope section and asks when the guest was born.

"September 20."

"Really? So you're right on the cusp. Let's see what they have to say about you." He proceeds to read what's in store for the guest, much like an older brother teaching his sibling one of life's essential lessons while sitting on the curb beside the local candy shop. At the end of his recital he says, "It's all in fun, of course, but you'd be surprised how much of this stuff actually comes true."

Palmer is at his scattershot best whenever he's given free rein to reminisce about his career. On a rare slow morning in his Vancouver office in June 2013, he spends an hour telling stories that shaped or reinforced his approach to business. At this stage his biographer has known him for several months and is no longer disoriented when Palmer jumps from one topic to the next. At least, not completely. Somehow each unrelated story is part of a bigger, cohesive picture.

Long before Palmer's entry into the ad world, when he was still a teenager working at the bakery, one of his jobs was to package bread that came down the production line. "It was standard practice to put the same bread in different packages, because it would be going to different retailers," he recalls. "One day while shopping in a grocery I came across a woman who was holding one of my loaves, and when she noticed me noticing her she informed me the loaf tasted far better than the breads in other stores.

"I couldn't help it; I told her it was actually the same bread. And you should have seen the expression of outrage on her face.

'Not so,' she replied, 'it's completely different. One bite and you can tell it's better.'

"I got hot under the collar too. 'Lady, I'm telling you, it's the same bread. I should know—I package the damn things.' But she refused to listen, so I said, 'Fine. You're right, the bread is different.'"

Palmer adds, "I guess that says a lot about the power of advertising. To this day I vividly recall how adamant that woman was about the superiority of her damned bread."

After a few minutes of casual conversation, the name of a famous Vancouver public relations man pops up: Thomas Butler. Starting in the 1960s and for more than thirty years, Butler practised public relations on a flamboyant scale. He handled visits of the likes of Charlton Heston, Billy Carter, Ginger Rogers and Neil Armstrong. One of his more outlandish ideas was to stage the World Belly Flop and Cannonball Diving Contest at the Bayshore and the Coach House Inn, which wound up getting American television network coverage.

Butler was responsible for the unveiling of the *Girl in a Wetsuit* sculpture at Stanley Park, and he also took a live beaver from the same park to New York, San Francisco and Los Angeles to promote convention travel in BC, a stunt that led to twenty new conventions worth millions coming to the city.

In the early 1970s Palmer was part owner of an ad agency undergoing a name change, and he was anxious to spread the news to as many potential clients as possible. Since Butler exerted considerable influence over the local press, Palmer figured a good word from him to *Vancouver Sun* columnist Jack Wasserman might result in the rebranded agency receiving positive ink. "So I phoned Tom, explained the situation and asked if he could do me a favour," he says. "Tom replied, 'If you want me to phone Jack, I'll see what

I can do.' Sure as hell, the very next week we were in Wasserman's column. It was great exposure, exactly what we needed."

A week after that Palmer received an envelope in the mail from Butler. "Inside was an invoice for $500," he recalls. "I almost fainted; back then $500 was a big sum of money. I figured it had to be a prank, so I phoned Tom—and quickly learned it wasn't. I started to complain about the fee, and Tom calmly replied, 'Frank, it took me thirty years to make that phone call.'"

Sobered, Palmer promptly paid the invoice. "That was my first real lesson in business," he says. "It was Tom's way of telling me you can't get things for free nor should you expect things for free, at least on a professional level."

The more he reminisces, the more Palmer's memories of his early years in advertising assume diamond-sharp clarity. "I said before that the 1960s was the decade when ad men first practised 'less is more,' a value I've tried to live up to for most of my career. The Vancouver agency that pushed this agenda most brilliantly was Cockfield, Brown & Co. I remember visiting their office on one occasion and being blown away by what they were doing."

Formed in 1928 by the merger of a Toronto ad agency and a Montreal firm, Cockfield Brown was the first Canadian agency to establish its own research department, staffed with psychologists and other people from the newly emerging social sciences. It was also the first "Liberal-friendly" agency, and its services were viewed as indispensable to the Liberal government (which openly sought its research expertise) in the 1930s.

Cockfield Brown's pioneer work in political marketing can't be underestimated. In 1944 it coordinated the first-ever opinion survey in an electoral district, as well as a national opinion survey to test the appeal of party slogans. That same year it also supervised forty-three opinion polls in Ontario electoral districts to assess Liberal support (the surveys represented the first use of polling by a Canadian political party).

By the time Palmer visited its Vancouver office, Cockfield Brown's fortunes were in a downward spiral, despite having secured a $6-million account to promote Expo 67—Montreal's International and Universal Exposition. But Palmer recalls the extraordinary talent of its people. "I saw their ad campaign for a paint company, and it consisted of just one line of copy and crisp, clean graphics," he says. "Everything had been boiled down to the essentials; there was absolutely no waste, no unnecessary frills. And better still, the campaign looked effortless. It had the kind of brevity all ad men were trying to accomplish for their clients."

When asked for an example of a campaign of his own that had lasting impact during the 1970s, Palmer doesn't hesitate to reply. "At Trend Advertising, which I became a partner of in 1969, we hired the actor Jackson Davies of *The Beachcombers* and got him to play this crazy, totally inept car salesman in a series of television ads for Carter Motors," he says. "Davies really made that character work. That material could have gone either way, but he made the salesman's ineptitude enormously funny instead of obnoxious."

When the ads were first produced, the Carter Motors people took Palmer aside and asked how long it would take before the ads had a positive effect on their sales. "I estimated that within nine months they would see an uptick, and I turned out to be correct," he says.

Galvanized by the memories of when he first appreciated the power of simplicity, Palmer rolls his chair over to his computer, punches a few keys and plays a YouTube video of an old television commercial produced by DDB's Chicago office. In it, a man slathers

Tabasco sauce on his pizza with every bite. A mosquito lands on his forearm, draws some blood and then flies away. As the man happily munches his Tabasco-infused pizza in the foreground, the mosquito recedes into the background—and then explodes in a cloud of hot vapour.

Palmer looks like a kid gazing at a toy store window. "Simple," he says reverently. "No words, great impact."

It's small wonder that one of Palmer's early inspirations was Keith Reinhard, who would later become CEO of DDB Worldwide. Born in 1935, Reinhard flexed his muscles during the golden days of US advertising and, as part of Needham, Harper & Steers in 1970, revolutionized McDonald's marketing campaigns. He did so by studying and sampling fast food and interviewing fast-food customers; this led him to conclude that people craved the emotional rewards of McDonald's food as much as the food itself, hence the immortal anthem (created by Reinhard) "You deserve a break today."

As head of DDB, Reinhard created Omnicom Group, and early on Palmer took Reinhard's often-repeated credo—"Agencies can't work too hard at understanding their clients' business"—to heart.

Palmer's love affair with simplicity has rubbed off on the younger generation of ad men, most notably (at least in Vancouver) Chris Staples, whose Rethink Communications has been called one of the most dynamic agencies in the country by Christopher Loudon, editor-in-chief of the trade publication *Marketing*. In 2009 when Staples was in his late forties, he told *BCBusiness* magazine writer Kevin Chong, "If I were to throw one ping-pong ball at you, you'd probably catch it. If I were to throw five at you at the same time, you'd probably catch none of them. Most ads have several ping-pong balls. There are too many messages in them."

McDonald's became a hugely important client for Palmer. "For twenty-seven years we handled their marketing in Western Canada," he says. "Vickers & Benson took care of McDonald's in Ontario, another firm handled it in Quebec, and Cossette was responsible for McDonald's overall operations in Canada."

Rivalry ebbed and flowed between the agencies over time, however, ultimately causing McDonald's to put all the accounts up for bid in the late 1990s. Palmer and his team resolved to create a pitch that would blow everyone else's out of the water, and they focused on what they perceived to be the restaurant's only short-coming. "Back then McDonald's coffee wasn't that good, so we decided to bring Juan Valdez himself from Colombia to Montreal, where we were supposed to deliver our pitch," he recalls.

Palmer quickly discovered that Juan Valdez was an actor named Carlos Sánchez. "There have been several of these ac-tors over the decades, but we got the one who was doing all the commercials at the time," he says. "Not only did we bring him to Montreal, we also brought along his mule, and when we introduced them to the crowd of McDonald's owner/operators, everyone went crazy! They thought it was the greatest thing ever. We didn't just blow them out of the water, we blew them into the stratosphere."

Palmer smiles at the memory. "Anyway, the moral of the story is we didn't win the business. In fact, we lost all of it. The whole damn account, after almost thirty years."

After pausing to let his unexpected punchline sink in, Palmer adds, "About ten years later we were told we actually did win the business, only someone decided to give it to someone else."

When he's asked to explain what he just said, Palmer's eye-brows rise in surprise: to his way of thinking, his discourse is never less than crystal clear. "Well, who knows what goes on behind closed doors? That's another fundamental aspect of advertising: many times you never find out the real reason you don't get certain accounts or lose others. Sometimes it's politics, sometimes it's a whim or just bad timing. My point is that wondering why can give you an ulcer. For me, it was good enough to know at the time that we blew these guys out of the water, and it was icing on the cake a decade later to be reminded of the fact."

Suddenly inspired to dig out a memento of the McDonald's pitch, Palmer rolls his chair over to a wall unit and rummages through drawers. Instead of finding what he wants, he comes across a drawer full of small red boxes, each labelled "Eviltron." Grinning, he opens one and pulls out a quarter-sized electronic device. "These things are so fucking funny it's unbearable," he says. He pushes a tiny button on the side of the device, and an ominous whisper emanates from it. He pushes the button again, and a malevolent voice snarls, "Can you hear me?"

Palmer slides his chair over to his desk. "See, this thing has a magnet, and what you do is attach it somewhere where nobody will notice: under a metal drawer or to the frame of a chair. Every several minutes the device will make a noise, and it drives people nuts!"

Palmer's glee is infectious, and the more his guests laugh, the more encouraged he is to test the device's different noises. "I'm glad I found these. I'm meeting with my DDB boss in New York next week: I think I'll plant one in his bathroom."

Not surprisingly, Palmer has a funny story about DDB and McCann Erickson, the global advertising agency whose roots date back to 1902, when Alfred Erickson formed his own ad agency in New York City (during the early 1970s the company was responsible for imprinting the deathless jingle "I'd like to teach the world to sing" in the minds of television viewers across North America).

McCann was one of the powerhouses that expressed an interest in buying Palmer Jarvis Communications in the late 1990s. "By that time, several high-power agencies that had expressed an interest in buying me also treated me like shit, simply because we were a small, Western Canadian player, and McCann was no different," Palmer says. "I flew all the way to New York to meet John Dooner, who was then McCann's chairman and CEO, and once I got to his office I had to wait in reception for forty-five minutes before he came out. When he finally did, he walked over to me, checked his watch and informed me he only had twenty minutes of time."

Palmer shakes his head disgustedly. "That was the equivalent of saying, 'Fuck you.' So I waited until he delivered his speech, thanked him for his time and left. Anyway, flash forward many years to a New York bar, where I was having drinks with Omnicom chairman John Wren. Wren told me John Dooner was coming to his office the next day to discuss business. So I suggested we play a joke on him, and Wren was all for it.

"The next morning when Dooner walks into Wren's office, I'm there too, innocently sipping a coffee. Wren says to him, 'You remember Frank, don't you?' Dooner looks at me for a moment and shakes his head. Wren says, 'He's the guy whose agency you considered buying years ago.' Suddenly Dooner remembers, and before he can react Wren walks over to him and takes his hand in both of his, a big grin on his face. 'I've got to tell, you,' he says, 'I'm so glad you never bought Frank, because I did and he's been making a fortune for me ever since!'"

At this point Palmer's guests half expect him to burst out laughing, but instead he is savouring the recollection of Dooner turning sheet-white. "That was a great and well-deserved 'Fuck you' right back, and the best part was I didn't even need to do it.

"I'm pretty easygoing, but I don't like being treated badly, especially when there's no reason for it. If that happens, chances are I won't get angry or throw furniture around. But I will find a way to get back at you, no matter how long it takes."

Question: Do you think of yourself as a remarkable person or someone easily forgettable?

Tough question to answer, isn't it? We would all like to believe we are remarkable. I know that when I've gone to a party or attended a business meeting, someone has always stood out from the rest of the crowd: someone who dressed better, was friendlier and exhibited a spark that garnered everyone's attention. These individuals always seem to get ahead in life, especially in business.

In our daily business at the agency, clients like solid, professional, friendly, trusting relationships. They want to be around people who stand out from others and are fun to be around. The same applies whether it's an employer seeking new talent or someone trying to get the attention of another person for a date.

So how do we become remarkable? The short answer is, don't blend in with the crowd. Here are some pointers that might help you to become remarkable.

Don't act like everyone else. I don't mean act like a jerk or wear something outlandish. I mean, be uniquely yourself in style and personality. Be comfortable in your own skin. Becoming someone who gets noticed might mean taking a small risk and living a little on the edge. You have to be that person who is willing to do something that others can't predict.

In our business, you can count the individuals and agencies that stand out on the fingers of one hand. And for the most part they are more successful and more in demand. So if you wish to be unforgettable, start working on being more remarkable—and take a risk or two.

—FRANK PALMER

CHAPTER FOUR

Frank Sharpens His Pencils

Before universities began turning trades into professions, reporters were smug in their conviction that they could control the actions of their readers. Ad men were even bolder: they felt as if they controlled people's minds.

Palmer and his friends will be the first to admit that this sentiment usually manifested itself during a long night of drinking or on completing a particularly tough ad campaign. It surfaced fleetingly but intensely, a mental reward for investing endless hours in creating products that were clever and influential but ultimately ephemeral.

The sentiment was also a small compensation for being in a trade that, then as now, earned its fair share of brickbats. After all, in the early decades of the twentieth century the acceptable thing for young folk to do was follow friends or family into a legitimate trade, like plumbing or contracting, or go to university and become a doctor or lawyer. The advertising business was a vaguely seedy enterprise whose practitioners, like their journalistic brethren, seemed to have congregated out of necessity, or for a lark or because (so the common perception went) they had attempted other careers and failed.

Palmer says, "On the one hand, my parents never tried to push me into a profession like law or medicine—largely because we were working class and that kind of world was beyond our reach.

"On the other hand, it wouldn't have been a surprise to some people back then if I'd followed in my dad's footsteps and worked at a bread company all my life. This was never in the cards as far as I was concerned, but convictions don't always correlate with outcomes."

Many powerful ad men gravitated to advertising by accident, such as David Ogilvy, who in his early years eked out a living as a chef in Paris and a social worker in the Edinburgh slums. It was only after he wrote an instruction manual for other salesmen about how to sell stoves that the ad world noted his talent and reeled him in. "My boyhood hero had been Lloyd George, and I had expected to become prime minister when I grew up," he wrote in his 1963 autobiography, *Confessions of an Advertising Man*. "Instead, I finally became an advertising agent on Madison Avenue; the revenues of my nineteen clients are now greater than the revenue of Her Majesty's Government."

Some great ad men were originally reporters (a profession that Palmer, incidentally, views with equal measures of respect and distrust). Leo Burnett plied the trade during the first two decades of the twentieth century until he realized the enormous growth potential of the ad world and got a job editing an in-house publication for Cadillac dealers (this led to him becoming an advertising director for the company).

Vancouver broadcaster Red Robinson became an ad man in the 1960s partly because he didn't like the ad copy he was obliged to read on the radio. "I was always rewriting the ads because I didn't think they were as effective as they could be," he says. "In fact, a great many of them missed the point. So when CFUN, the radio station I was program director for, was sold out from under me in 1967, I decided to launch my own agency: Trend Advertising."

Robinson admits that his main goal was to keep putting food on the family table. "I had no money, just a mortgage, a wife and three kids. That was enough inspiration for me to make Trend a success."

Still other famous ad men started out as commercial artists. This was Frank Palmer's background and that of his early mentor, Keith Reinhard, who is now Chairman Emeritus of DDB Worldwide. In a 2012 interview published on the DDB Worldwide website, Reinhard recalled, "I grew up in rural Indiana and became fascinated with advertising and brands at an early age. I particularly remember examining the countless ads plastered on the walls of the local grocery store where my mom worked when I would go there to help her out.

"I loved advertising with a passion and took a correspondence course in commercial art, and since I couldn't afford college, I then interned at a commercial art studio. Later I got a job in a big commercial art studio in Chicago." Reinhard subsequently worked with comics such as Jack Benny, George Carlin, Don Adams and Dick Cavett.

As Palmer has stated, he grew up in a household in which his mother played practical jokes and managed her husband's take-home pay. Aside from vowing to control his own purse strings when he got older, Palmer claims to have had a happy childhood; his after-school work routine at McGavin's bakery with his father Russell was offset by summer fun at Kitsilano Beach, and his hatred of school was nullified by the money he made at the bakery. "To be fair, there were enjoyable aspects about school," he says. "I was known as the artist, and I enjoyed designing the yearbooks, posters and graphics they needed for various things around Kitsilano High."

His childhood friend Brian Robertson, who today is a Vancouver mortgage broker, recalls Palmer as being "extremely outgoing, girl-crazy and, yes, an artist. None of his friends, me included, could imagine he would ever enter the business world, let alone achieve the degree of success he now enjoys. He seemed too artsy for the corporate scene."

When he wasn't working or being a beach bum, Palmer was sketching and swiping his mother Phyllis's petits fours, which she made for a local restaurant. "To this day if I see petits fours at a wedding or some other social event, I can't pass them by," he says. "I could eat a hundred of them."

The Vancouver of the 1940s and '50s that Palmer grew up in was exciting in terms of its media development and physical expansion. In 1944 Bill Rea started the radio station CKNW, which had hourly newscasts around the clock and also introduced a late-night disc jockey named Jack Cullen: elements that no other radio station could lay claim to. In 1948, a handful of Vancouverites who owned small, bulbous transmission screens received Vancouver's first television signal: a college football game played in Seattle (five years later the city would have its own television station when CBUT, the CBC's local channel, went on the air).

During the 1950s commercial jet aircraft became commonplace, which opened up more flights across the Pacific and in turn necessitated an expansion of the Vancouver airport. Suburbia also expanded, resulting in the building of more bridges and a tunnel to link Vancouver to the rest of the rapidly evolving Lower Mainland.

Palmer was in his teens when Vancouver became ground zero for two new Canadian phenomena: the opening of the Park Royal shopping centre (the country's first indoor mall) and an industrial park on Annacis Island. Consumerism expanded too: the six-day shopping week was introduced, and Vancouver's first cocktail bar (in the Sylvia Hotel) opened for business. Clearly, Vancouver was looking toward the future.

But the youthful Palmer rarely thought of his future; too much was going on in the present, and one focus was his growing penchant for pulling gags. An early joke that got him in the most trouble involved feeding his father a peanut butter sandwich laced with laxative prior to a shift at McGavin's. "That evening we were placing the freshly baked bread on racks, and it was policy that if you needed to go to the bathroom, you had to raise your hand in front of everyone and the foreman would excuse you," Palmer recalls.

Shortly after he began his shift Russell raised his hand, was excused and hurried to the lavatory. Several minutes later he returned to his post, but no sooner did he resume handling the loaves than with some urgency he raised his hand again. The foreman nodded, and Russell dashed to the toilet. "He came back to his post, resumed work and then raised his hand yet again," says Palmer, almost choking with laughter. "This went on for hours! When he found out I was behind it, he almost killed me. He actually chased me around the dining room table. I'm lucky to still be alive."

It's interesting to note that this specific memory is a touchstone of sorts for Palmer, something that pops into his head and never fails to lighten his mood. A typical example of this occurred one afternoon in his DDB office: after a series of lengthy and unpleasant business calls to New York, and after uttering a long string of obscenities and slamming the receiver onto its cradle several times, Palmer reclined in his chair and looked out his window. Within a few minutes he was chuckling to himself. Glancing up at his baffled assistant, he explained, "I was just thinking about the time I fed my father his Ex-Lax sandwich!"

Brian Robertson clearly admires Palmer's facility for working and playing hard. "He worked like a dog, but he never passed up the opportunity to have fun at the same time, and that served him well later on," he says.

Robertson recalls his friendship with Palmer while dining at a trendy Vancouver eatery, with one hand on an ice-cold beer and the other seeking the forearm of a pretty waitress (who playfully but firmly slaps it away). "Our Friday nights were spent carousing at the Ridge Theatre. That is, until Frank detonated a stink bomb and cleared out the joint. He also loved fancy automobiles. One time we were driving to the local White Spot in his customized '48 Chevy, and he was preening and looking cool. Unfortunately a pretty girl passed by, which caused him to smash into the car ahead of him. The entire front end of the Chevy was trashed."

Robertson retains a special fondness for Palmer's mother. "Phyllis was a great lady," he says. "She was mom to all the neighbourhood kids, and her devotion to Frank did a lot to shape him as a person. Russell was more passive, but he too gave Frank a strong sense of purpose thanks to his work ethic."

Russell was also a pragmatist, sometimes harshly so, a trait that rubbed off on Palmer. One time the family was sitting at the dining table eyeing three freshly cooked steaks of different sizes. Without a word Russell reached over, skewered the biggest one and deposited it on his plate, much to the indignation of his wife. Palmer says, "He asked her what she would have done. She said, 'I would have taken the small steak.' And he replied, 'Then what are you bitching about? You got what you wanted.'"

To what degree Russell influenced his son's ruthless streak is unclear, but Palmer often tells the story of how Russell used to take him to the movies and then on the way back buy a brick of ice cream. When they got home, Russell would slice the brick open, cut his son a piece that was no bigger than a quarter and eat the rest himself. "That always hurt me, but I didn't have the nerve to tell him so until decades later when he was on his deathbed," says Palmer. "What I didn't appreciate was that Dad came from a family of eleven kids, and if he didn't take what he wanted, he didn't get anything."

Palmer tells this story to explain why he consciously chose to be more generous with people than Russell had been. Those acquainted with Palmer suspect it helps explain his determination to get what he wants no matter the cost.

Still others take the significance of Palmer's often-repeated stories with a grain of salt. With a curious mixture of fondness and exasperation, Hilary Robertson remarks, "Oh, Frank and his bloody ice-cream story."

Marika Palmer, who has heard all the stories and then some, discloses that her husband has been unable to let go of some of the negative early emotions that brewed during his childhood. "He has a lot of fear that he keeps well hidden. Some, like his fear of winding up homeless, truly terrify him even though at this point there's little logic to it.

"But I think the childhood memory that has remained the most vivid in his mind is Phyllis grabbing Russell's paycheques. Frank's obsession with money, with control and being generous with other people all stem from that incident. It's interesting to speculate what kind of man he would have turned into had he not witnessed that ritual."

Regardless of Russell's shortcomings, Palmer acknowledges, almost enviously, that Russell and Phyllis were deeply devoted to each other: "Dad was eleven years older than Mom, but she died first, at sixty-nine, of a brain tumour, and he died at eighty-one of leukemia. But if you ask me, I think Dad really died because he was so dependent on Mom."

George Jarvis thinks it's important to consider that Frank was an only child and his parents doted on him. "To what extent this shaped his ambitions I can't say, but I would guess that Frank was never told—at least not by Russell or Phyllis—that he couldn't succeed at anything he undertook. I think Frank grew up assuming he would be a success at anything he decided to do, and that combined with the work ethic, made him formidable."

If subconscious fears also contribute to a strong work ethic, then a childhood incident involving Vancouver's Burrard Bridge stokes Palmer's compulsion to keep busy at an age when most men are well into retirement. "I was playing hide and seek with a buddy at the bridge, and at one point I managed to break through a locked door at the bridge's base," he recalls. "Inside it was pitch dark, but I stepped in and started walking. I literally couldn't see my hands in front of me, and then something made me stop, bend over and rummage around for a stone. I tossed it ahead of me, and about ten seconds later I heard a splash from far below."

To this day Palmer occasionally sits bolt upright in bed in a cold sweat, having dreamed yet again that he has plummeted into the water.

*   *   *

Palmer summarizes his early scholastic achievements: "I failed grade one due to asthma and grade ten because I was working at multiple bakeries and running multiple bread-making machines. I was a 'jobber' for the union, and my eventual graduation from high school couldn't have come quickly enough. There was no money to be made in school. I thought it was a colossal waste of time."

But with an eye toward being a commercial artist, Palmer spent two and a half years diligently studying at the Vancouver Art School (now the Emily Carr University of Art + Design). "I worked with clay, I learned silk screening and I painted, all with the objective of eventually making a living designing logos," he says.

He soon realized, however, that "most of my teachers or professors had something going on the side. They were doing freelance work outside of the art school, and it was obvious they were more interested in that than teaching." Nonetheless, Palmer was compensated for his time in academe by meeting his first wife, Kathy, on campus.

An unquenchable curiosity about how the world works defines the mindset of the best ad men, and Palmer is no exception.

It helps explain why he would consider sacrificing his burgeoning commercial art skills to pursue a career in law enforcement; after leaving Vancouver Art School in 1961 he took a Vancouver Police Department entry exam.

When pressed to explain his thinking, Palmer struggles to conjure the right words. "I guess I was attracted to the idea of being in a position of power and authority," he says. "And I've always loved getting behind the scenes. Plus, I was physically ideal for the job. In any event, I passed the physical and other requirements but failed the psychological part of the exam, so I had no hope of becoming a cop. I found out years later from a recruiter that the examiners failed me because they suspected I wouldn't be able to take orders."

Shortly afterward came a turning point in Palmer's life, when Ken Davidson of the Vancouver office of kvos television station examined his portfolio and hired him as an artist in the advertising/sales department.

Although licensed in Bellingham, Washington, and nominally part of the Seattle market, kvos, which signed on in 1953, primarily served Southwestern BC audiences. Its first broadcast was of Elizabeth II's coronation, which ensured its place in the annals of Canadian broadcasting. Since Canada had no television stations west of Ontario at the time, BBC's coverage of the event was shipped to Vancouver by air; from there, Mounties drove it to the border and handed it to the Washington State Patrol, who then drove the film to Bellingham.

During the years Palmer worked for kvos and later honed his talent as a fledgling ad man, kvos produced a variety of local shows. The religious program *Anchor* first aired in 1968, with host Pastor Len Ericksen, and ran for thirty years. The careers of Andy

Anderson and Al Swift, who later became successful politicians, were launched with the help of programming such as *The 10:30 Report*, *Weeks End* and *Cana West*. Red Robinson later hosted *Red's Classic Theatre*, from 1989 to 2001.

KVOS proved to be a training ground for gaining skills that Palmer could only dream about at school and that would prepare him for the technical demands of the ad world. For the next five years he happily jumped from one job to another within the station. "I was making $500 a month and thought I'd gone to heaven," he says.

Palmer painted the Indian faces displayed in the "Sorry for the interruption" logos that occasionally disrupted broadcasting. "Also, the station's retail clients who bought airtime from us received window banners, shelf talkers, and other advertising material for their business, and I was responsible for doing the artwork for these items," he says.

* * *

Since KVOS also aided in the production of several budget-conscious Hollywood television cartoon series via its Canarim division, Palmer found himself colouring animation cels for Hanna-Barbera's *Jonny Quest* as well as *The Beatles* (the latter was produced mainly by Artransa Park Studios in Sydney, Australia, and TVC Animation in London, England).

When he wasn't painting cels, Palmer was learning how to burn plates and process negatives. "KVOS was a wonderful factory," he says. "The cel colouring was done in two small houses, and the printing presses were located on the top storey of the main KVOS building, and because a good portion of local television back then was still live, you had to learn quickly and get jobs done even quicker." By the time Palmer left KVOS in 1965, he was in all senses of the title a qualified production manager.

The work ethic that governed Palmer's childhood enabled him to blaze through twelve-hour days and then visit people unrelated to KVOS who needed design work done. "I would spend the night designing letterheads and logos, and drop them off in the morning before returning to KVOS," he recalls. "It got to the point where the money I was making on the side was bigger than my salary at the station, and it never seemed like a strain because I was always coming up with better and quicker ways to get things done."

To Palmer's chagrin technological improvements rendered much of what he had learned in art school obsolete. "All that painting and silk screening was with the intention of becoming a good logo artist, which back then required enormous precision. I spent endless hours drawing type, to the point where I got double vision," he says. "But when Letraset was invented in 1959 and became mainstream in the 1960s, that innocuous product influenced the production process just as powerfully as computers did decades later."

Vancouver still harboured a good number of residents who took perverse pride in being isolated from the rest of Canada by virtue of being west of the Rockies, but the city was furiously playing catch-up with other urban centres. In 1960 it got its first independent television station, to the delight of metropolitan Vancouver's total population of over 800,000 (double the figure of just twenty years earlier, according to The History of Metropolitan Vancouver website). Highway 401 (better known today as the Trans-Canada Highway) extended its reach to the city and farther west. Culture took a giant step forward with the opening of the Queen Elizabeth Playhouse, and people could communicate with each other more easily with the advent of direct dialing. The introduction of bathtub races (in which contestants raced from Nanaimo to Vancouver's Kitsilano beach in modified powered bathtubs as part of Vancouver's annual Sea Festival) and the founding of Greenpeace in a Dunbar neighbourhood living room enhanced Vancouver's reputation as an oddball Mecca.

Amid this bustle and his busy schedule, Palmer still found time to pull pranks. "Marriage didn't slow him down, and nothing has changed in the intervening years," says Brian Robertson. "If we were at a hotel and he saw a pretty woman sunbathing by the pool, he would pay a kid a quarter to spill ice water on her. He once laced Hilary Robertson's coffee cup with the substance dentists used to freeze gums; her mouth was so numb she couldn't make herself understood to incoming callers."

Hilary Robertson bursts out laughing when reminded of the incident. "I could have strangled Frank because I was convinced I was having a stroke. But at the same time it was funny, and you couldn't help but laugh, because whenever he pulled one of his corny gags his fat head would pop up from around a corner or from under a table, grinning from ear to ear."

The pranks became more elaborate with each passing year. "Frank's son and daughter weren't spared," says Brian Robertson. "One time he wired their teddy bears so they could move via remote control; he must have spent hours setting that up." Corporate boardrooms were especially popular targets. "During a meeting with *Vancouver Sun* columnist Malcolm Parry and other journalists, Frank had a remote-control fart machine that, when activated, sounded like the farts were coming right out of Malcolm's ass."

Decades later, Hugh Ruthven would comment on Palmer's antics: "Frank dislikes many things, but aging would be at the top of his list. Once, when he was in his sixties, he told me in all seriousness, 'I don't hang out with people my age because they're too old.'

"Frank doesn't act his age because he has no idea how old he is. He's not an old guy trying to be hip, he's a twenty-four-year-old with an extra forty-four years of knowledge that he has tucked away."

If Brian Robertson took delight in the fact that a big part of Palmer never grew up, he was even more impressed by Palmer's evolving business skills, which he first noticed in 1971 when Palmer sold him the house he had bought for himself and Kathy in 1968.

Robertson notes that Palmer had originally purchased the house for $18,000, but his selling price was $30,000. "This was the start of the buying and selling of real estate that continues to this day. Frank buys impulsively, but he's got an awfully sharp eye."

With so much going on, did Palmer at any time during his KVOS stint entertain the idea of a career as an ad man? "No," he replies. "I was too busy working to see ahead. It was all about making a living as a young married man." Arguably, were it not for doing design work at KVOS on behalf of Red Robinson, Palmer might never have committed himself fully to the ad business.

In the 1960s Robinson was famous as the first disc jockey to regularly play rock and roll over the airwaves in Canada. He had enjoyed success in the 1950s as a guest host on CBC Television's *Cross-Canada Hit Parade*, and became one of only two entertainers to ever emcee for Elvis Presley and the Beatles (in 1957 and 1964, respectively).

When Robinson launched Trend Advertising in 1967, he quickly distinguished himself by focusing on ad campaigns for the broadcast medium. "Even though the 1960s weren't so long ago, it was a completely different world," he recalls. "Back then, the newspapers controlled everything and were the focus of most local ad agencies. The prevailing wisdom was that you couldn't make any money off regional retail advertising—or at least that was the assumption of the big agencies out east that had all the big clients, moribund as they were with bureaucracy."

Convinced that broadcast advertising, like radio itself, could contribute to the "theatre of the mind" if properly executed, Robinson developed a list of clients that included Eagle Ford, Better Value Furniture (the forerunner of Stacey's Furniture) and the record division of RCA.

During this time Vancouver businessmen George Tidball and Herb Capozzi acquired the rights to the McDonald's franchise in Canada. They persuaded Robinson to visit one of the restaurants in Seattle in the hopes he would create an advertising campaign to launch the company locally. "I did so and was fascinated with what I saw," Robinson recalls. "There was no jukebox, no place to hang out and a limited menu. The burgers cost nineteen cents, you ordered your meal and then you departed. When I returned to Vancouver, George and Herb asked me to share my impressions. I told them, 'I like everything I saw, but I honestly don't know if I can work for a clown.'"

Tidball and Capozzi opened the first McDonald's in Canada on Richmond's No. 3 Road and soon after followed it with an outlet on Vancouver's Marine Drive. Robinson wrote and appeared in the first McDonald's television ad in Canada: "In the ad I said, in reference to the cost of purchasing a McDonald's meal, 'Isn't it good to get change back from your dollar?'" Robinson grins. "It was great fun and the ads were a success, but none of us could imagine how huge McDonald's would become."

Shortly after taking University of British Columbia student Rich Simons under his wing, Robinson was again approached by Tidball with a US coupon for McDonald's Filet-O-Fish burger. "He needed a similar coupon geared toward the Canadian market, and he needed fifty thousand of them in a hurry," he says. "Well, I knew nothing about the print business, but I knew the owner of Western Direct Mail and promptly paid him a visit."

As fortune would have it, Palmer had left KVOS for what would become a four-year stint as production manager for Western Direct Mail, which he describes as "a business that provided personalized products such as letterheads and logos to various clients. The job paid more than KVOS, and it was a good chance for me to further my printing abilities and artwork."

Robinson says, "I was at Western Direct explaining to the owner what I needed for the Filet-O-Fish coupons. I said, 'Is this something you can do?' and he replies, 'Yeah,' and shouts, 'Hey, Frank!' And in through a set of heavy plastic curtains separating the print shop from the office walked Frank Palmer. With the plastic curtains and his big build he reminded me of a butcher coming out of the back room after cutting up meat."

Palmer remembers the assignment vividly. "I designed and printed the Filet-O-Fish coupons, but at the time it was just another job to complete within a tight deadline. I did, however, like Red enormously."

The feeling was mutual. "I liked Frank from the start," says Robinson. "He was a character—you could tell that right away. He had a wicked sense of humour and he was a talented artist."

Palmer maintained his professional association with Robinson and Simons. "I moonlit for them and did an awful lot of their creative stuff. I told them on more than one occasion, 'I think you guys need a production manager and an artist inside, because both of you are capable of selling but you also need someone capable of doing.'"

*   *   *

Red Robinson's position in the local ad world was assured thanks to McDonald's, but the diehard broadcaster wanted to return to the medium he loved best. So at the end of the decade when Jim Pattison, then the executive responsible for CJOR, approached him about becoming program manager for the radio station, Robinson seized the opportunity. "However, Pattison insisted I focus exclusively on broadcasting, so I wound up selling my agency to Rich Simons for a dollar," he says. "I also suggested to Rich that he make Frank a partner."

Palmer jumped at the offer and officially became an ad man on April 1, 1969, the same year his son Darren was born. "I'd wanted my own business for a long time and I liked Trend," he says. "Plus, I'd been working double shifts in order to make decent money, and here was a chance to make even more." Palmer was just twenty-nine years old, armed with an unusual degree (even back then) of practical work experience.

Trend was a small agency located at 1350 East Georgia Street. "We traded our creative services for the office rent in a crappy little two-level building, that's how small we were," Palmer laughs. "But we were busy and nimble; we did a bit of TV, a bit of radio and a lot of print. We had a Mercury car dealership, Belmont Motors, an audio-visual firm and other local businesses as clients, and this was the decade when ads had become clean and clever. I was suddenly part of a very small group of Vancouver ad men who were all trying to outdo each other in providing memorable catch lines, images and slogans."

Dean Mailey, president and owner of Fusion Communications Group Inc., vividly recalls the Jackson Davies television ads for Carter Motors. "They were great, but Frank didn't stop there," he says. "He rented out billboards and plastered Davies's photo on them—upside down. Back then, this kind of advertising was cutting edge, and it made a huge impression on people. That's typical of what Frank would do, and it's also typical of the times."

Dealing with local clients could be challenging. Recalling Budget Brake & Muffler, Palmer says, "I'd have to wait for hours sometimes while they put a muffler on a car before I could get information for the ad we wanted to do on their behalf."

Then as now, Palmer tends not to dwell on his relationship with Simons, but others describe it as one in which the latter worked the former especially hard. In a rare moment of disclosure Palmer says, "I was the backroom guy, Rich was the sales guy and we were both good at what we did. But I do remember one time when Rich asked me to design a logo overnight on top of every-thing else I was doing, which was considerable. I designed the damned logo, but after going home I started getting the shakes and chest pains. I thought I was having a heart attack, but instead it was hypertension and I wound up spending two days in hospital because of it."

Trend took on Robin Lecky as a partner and in 1972 was re-branded Simons Palmer and Lecky (which prompted Palmer to solicit media attention from Thomas Butler, much to Palmer's un-

expected expense). The agency was on the road to achieving billings in excess of $1.5 million, a feat helped along by Rich Simons's
business skills, which included a background in the manufacturing and high-tech sectors (after stepping down as senior partner
in 1975, Simons went on to form the highly successful Simons
Advertising agency).

As for Robin Lecky, his talent for project and event-related
management led him, years later, to direct major campaigns for
four World Expositions and an Olympic Games. Palmer says,
"Working with these men taught me the importance of surround-
ing yourself with good people. I may not be the sharpest pencil in
the box, but I made damned sure in subsequent years to recruit
and surround myself with folk who were."

On that note Palmer pulls himself back into the present, suddenly fixated on discussing the importance of teams. It's been a
task for him to discuss his early career days in a linear fashion,
and making a point about teams now takes precedence, partly
because "team" is one of the most overused terms in the corporate
world—and for the independent-minded it signifies a haven for
people who can't excel on their own rather than professionals
who pool their talent to create excellence.

Palmer uses an analogy to describe what true teamwork is
in the ad world: the Blue Angels, the US Navy's flight acrobatic
squadron that thrills millions of spectators at air shows throughout North America. "They set the standard for teamwork," he says.
"Precision acrobatics of this calibre requires enormous singularity
of purpose, in addition to incredible talent and organizational
skills. One wrong move, and it's disaster."

Comparing the dangers of airborne acrobats to the hazards
of the ad world may be overly dramatic, but Palmer has found

it useful when he gives speeches to CEOs. "It's tough to inspire people at the top to do something other than win for themselves, so I use analogies like the Blue Angels or runners passing the baton to each other in a race," he says. "If you're the leader of a company, of any type of company, then everything people do must be for the greater good, the CEOs included. Otherwise, that company will suffer.

"In my experience, the only reason I'm known today is because of my partners and the people I worked with. The same goes for the other big names of the ad world. The achievements attributed to them may have been largely their doing, but they wouldn't have happened without enormous support and collaboration."

E ver thought about what you'd say about yourself if you were asked to buy a magazine?

What would your informal résumé state? I composed one for myself the other night:

Name: Frank Palmer

Age: 35 in his mind, acts 18

Title: Chairman/CEO DDB Canada

What's the first thing you do in the morning? Open email, and see how my wife and dog are.

Where do you get your news? I read at least four newspapers: *The Globe and Mail, Financial Post, Vancouver Sun, New York Times*. I check online *Adweek, Ad Age, Marketing Online*.

What books and magazines do you read? Anything about leadership and the advertising business. But I also admit to reading *us*, *People* and a few gossip magazines.

What are your go-to social media platforms? I normally don't use them. I don't wish to have a million friends or followers. In real life you are lucky if you have a handful of really good friends.

What's your favourite app? Uber, Shazam, autoTRADER.ca, TED, YouTube. It's hard to keep up with them all.

What TV shows do you watch? I love *True Detective* and *Breaking Bad*. Netflix is the best way to watch all the series, especially some of the British shows. I can watch two to four series in a row. I'm a TV addict.

What upsets you? People who only think of themselves. People who are always late for meetings. People who put other people down. People who are always on their cell phones and PCs during meetings. People who never look you in the eye while talking to them.

What are your hobbies? I love to paint but don't do it as much as I'd like to. I like going to the gym.

How do you wind down at night? I'm always on call. What I mean is that my head never quite shuts down. Maybe it's on pause?

—FRANK PALMER

"By far the most aggressive of the local ad men"

"I first met Frank in 1971 when I was a salesman for Price Printing in Vancouver. He was an in-your-face kind of guy, gregarious and physically imposing. Several years later I became an ad man with his ex-partner Rich Simons, and the stories he told of his relationship with Palmer didn't give me a positive impression of the man."

So says Peter Fassbender, former mayor of Langley, BC, and the province's education minister at the time he was interviewed for *Let's Get Frank* in 2013. Fassbender had been charged with the unenviable task of fostering peace between two long-standing foes: the BC Public School Employers' Association and the Liberal government, but despite this Herculean assignment, he was happy to discuss Palmer and did so between cabinet meetings.

Fassbender entered the ad world during the early 1970s when he left Price Printing and joined Creative House. Unlike many of his colleagues, he distinguished himself as a low-key, happily married creature of habit (he and his wife Charlene were both raised in Surrey, graduated from Queen Elizabeth Secondary School and have been married for forty-five years).

Creative House was not a full-service company, meaning that although it created multimedia presentations for clients, it did not provide media planning or placement. Many of its clients were also clients of full-service agencies, which caused the latter to accuse practitioners like Fassbender of stealing work.

Fassbender was therefore not too surprised when one morning he received a phone call from Palmer. "Frank very politely asked what I was trying to accomplish by working for Creative House, and I told him I was just trying to survive," he recalls. "What followed was a fairly tense conversation. Frank wasn't at any point discourteous, but he made it clear he didn't like me communicating directly with his clients."

Despite feeling intimidated, Fassbender continued to conduct business as usual. "Vancouver was a small town with no head offices that dictated procedure, so all the ad people were battling each other for work," he says. "In my mind, the clients were entirely in their right to obtain different services from different companies, whether they were full-service or not."

In many ways Vancouver was indeed still a small town during the 1970s, despite the metropolitan population topping the one-million mark. Within the city's narrow confines, however, business was booming. Its economic links to the Pacific Rim were enhanced with the opening of a coal port at Delta's Roberts Bank. Whistler became a resort municipality in 1975 and a major lure for leisure travellers across the world. Local talent such as architect Arthur Erickson attracted international attention, specifically in 1979 when he unveiled the new courthouse and Robson Square complex in Vancouver's downtown core.

In 1975 the rivalry between Fassbender and Palmer intensi-fied when Fassbender left Creative House to join the full-service Simons Advertising agency, the latest addition to the already crowded Vancouver ad scene. "Naturally one of the first things I did was ask Rich Simons about his stint with Frank," he recalls. "To put it mildly, they hadn't seen eye to eye when they were running Simons Palmer and Lecky. They had conflicting ideas about how to conduct and build business. Plus, Rich was pretty straitlaced, so Frank's antics often irritated him.

"In any event, as a result of these disclosures I didn't form a positive opinion about Frank. It was obvious he was hell-bent on winning at any cost, and if he smelled blood he was all over it like a dirty shirt. He was by far the most aggressive of the local ad men, and now that he had evolved his business into Palmer Jarvis his reputation was near legendary, at least on the West Coast. I kind of feared him."

Fassbender chuckles and adds, "On a personal level we were profoundly different. Frank was the quintessential hard-drinking ad man, and with regard to the ladies he was also a bit of a hound dog. I was a married guy who loved nothing better than on Fridays to put the bright lights of Vancouver in my rear-view mirror and go home to my wife and kids in the peaceful Fraser Valley."

Over the years colleagues have appreciated how Frank the Hunter and Frank the Ladies' Man are intertwined. "Frank loves women so much because it's like chasing and landing a big account," Hugh Ruthven once wrote. "Once the race is on, Frank pulls out all the stops and will make any phone call or secret meeting happen in order to try to get the upper hand."

Ruthven went on to remark, "Don't bring a knife to a gunfight because Frank has no real rules in this game. Winner takes all, and Frank's first approach is always to try to charm and get as many people as possible to like him. This chase is to bring fame and more dollars to the agency, sure, but mostly it's about the love of the chase."

Fassbender wasn't shy about going after clients; he merely did so more subtly than Palmer, once even turning the tables on his rival. "I learned that Frank had sent his people out to Kelowna to try to steal away one of our clients, the juice beverage manufacturer SunRype," he says. "The SunRype people had just signed with us and had no intention of jumping ship, but after I found out that Frank had approached them by proxy, I couldn't resist phoning him and telling him, 'Nice try!' For once Frank was at a loss for words. He'd been caught with his hand in the cookie jar, and it was especially funny considering his phone call to me a few years prior, complaining about Creative House stealing work from his agency!

"So that's the kind of rivalry that existed back then. But it was a respectful rivalry, because early on I realized just how skilful an ad man Frank was. He had great intuition about what would work and what wouldn't. He was extremely focused, and he had the degree of commitment to the business that separates the great from the good. Plus, he had a knack for finding the very best talent and recruiting it.

"However, I was damned if I was going to lose any business to Frank Palmer—and I'll admit I called on his clients from time to time, McDonald's included." Fassbender and Simons ultimately generated billings in excess of $35 million with clients such as Kentucky Fried Chicken, Safeway Canada, and the federal and BC governments.

Simons Advertising and Palmer Jarvis grew steadily through-out the 1970s and '80s, and increasingly Fassbender found himself listening to Simons's ideas for fostering the next step of evolution. One day in 1988, Simons returned from a luncheon and called Fassbender into his office. "I've just had lunch with someone who might represent our future," he said.

"Oh, really? Who?"

"Frank Palmer."

Even though Simons uttered these words some twenty-five years ago, the hairs still stand out on Fassbender's neck as he relates them. "I was flabbergasted, and my jaw dropped," he says. "But Rich was perfectly calm and composed, as if he'd just met Frank for the first time instead of being a disgruntled ex-partner. As I sat there wondering if Rich had lost his mind, he informed me, 'Palmer Jarvis has a lot to offer us, and we have a lot to offer them, and merging with them makes perfect sense when you think about it.'

"Well, I couldn't believe it. I thought Rich was nuts. But he was adamant, so I met Frank for coffee in his office soon afterward to voice my skepticism about the whole idea. I wound up my brief speech by stating, 'On top of everything else, I'm not even sure if I like you, and in all probability you might not like me. So if we proceed with the merger, we both need to be honest with each other and admit if it's working or not.' Frank absorbed this, then he smiled that small, sly smile of his and replied, 'Well, that's about as honest an approach to business as anyone could hope for.'"

Such is the loopy social world of the ad industry that shortly after the merger it was Fassbender, not Simons, who settled snugly into the Palmer Jarvis culture. "I think Rich proceeded with the merger because he knew it would be good for everyone in our company."

Hilary Robertson became Simons's executive assistant after joining the agency in 1988, and she doesn't mince words recounting the experience: "I didn't like Rich at all, but I was in my late twenties and new to the game, so I kept my mouth shut."

Whenever Palmer visited Simons's office to discuss business, he would stop along the way to chat with Robertson in her adjoining office. "And that drove Rich crazy," she recalls. "I think he regarded it as undermining his authority. At one point he even told me, 'Don't discuss anything about me with Palmer.' Frank soon sensed that his visits were getting on Rich's nerves, so he visited even more frequently and then started closing the door of my office whenever he dropped by—which sent Rich over the edge."

Simons ultimately left the agency and spent ten years in the United States as a business builder. He moved back to Vancouver in 2001 and became president and CEO of RewardStream Inc., a leading application service provider for customer loyalty and reward programs.

Fassbender was hard-pressed to imagine a more productive organization in which to ply his trade than Palmer Jarvis. "We each had different specialties and a client roster that suited our talents," he says. "I had all of the federal government accounts, plus I did a lot of social marketing; we were the first agency to put those 'shock' photos on the side of cigarette packages. Frank had McDonald's, and we were always exchanging ideas and inspiring each other."

Fassbender agrees with Palmer that the ad world was more fun back then compared with today. "Decisions were made independently, personal risks were taken and everything moved like lightning," he says. "There were no corporate restraints. The intense pace took its toll, but at the same time it was exhilarating."

Dean Mailey explains a key difference between plying the trade back then and now. "What the young ad men of today who answer to shareholders don't realize is that in the old days it was the ad man's money on the line. Yes, Frank and George Jarvis were relentless in sniffing for blood and going in for the kill when it came to getting clients, because it was their money and their reputation at risk.

"Frank has often described the ad world as full of hunters or farmers. Thirty years ago it was mostly hunters in the business, and this bolstered their creativity in many ways, not just in the realm of creating the ad campaigns. For example, Frank is the best pitch guy in Canada; he will stand in a room full of clients and make them believe that the marketing strategy he is proposing is absolutely brilliant and the only possible solution."

For the record, this is not a talent that Chris Staples embraces. He has frequently stated that his entire career has been a reaction to the television drama series *Mad Men*, which depicted the advertising industry—and its players—as less than ethical. "Instead, I'm a strong believer that today's practitioners should be judged on results, not the amount of dinners they take their clients to," he says.

In the interest of fairness, a suitable rebuttal to Staples's comment comes from Palmer himself. "I have no problem dining with clients, and I do it all the time—but I do it because I'm confident that we're doing a good job on their behalf. I fully agree that wining and dining doesn't make up for being less than professional at your job."

Palmer says socializing is an inextricable part of his business, plus as a people person he thoroughly enjoys luncheons and dinners with clients: "It's not only a way to learn about each other, it's a great way to build trust. The proof of this is that many agencies retain clients for eighteen months or so, but we have a long track record of clients who were with us for years, even decades, including McDonald's and SunRype."

Even though Fassbender enjoyed the bucolic life while Palmer caroused, or sipped juice while Palmer downed Chivas Regal, he found himself admiring Palmer on a personal level. Incidents such as the Woodward's department store bankruptcy in 1993 nurtured this sentiment. "Woodward's was our account, and when it went under we were on the hook for three-quarters of a million dollars of advertising paid for and committed to," he explains. "I'll never forget Frank telling me, 'We're in this for the long haul, so we have to take care of the local media.'

"He went to all the radio stations and newspapers and promised that if they gave him some time, he would pay them back in full out of his own pocket. And he proceeded to do so. Many people were so impressed that they accepted fifty cents on the dollar, and Palmer Jarvis wound up earning enormous respect that continues today under DDB."

Fassbender laughs when reminded that Palmer's stunt of bringing the actor who played Juan Valdez and his mule to a meeting with McDonald's owner/operators wasn't enough to keep that coveted account. "Yes, losing McDonald's had a huge impact on us. But fortunately, Frank was already diversifying the agency. So for every disaster there seemed to be an upside; for example, shortly after the Woodward's debacle we won a $30-million federal government contract to help launch the new Goods and Services Tax in the business community. That was the ad world back then: every time we thought we would die of a heart attack, our bacon would be saved at the last minute."

Somewhat wistfully, Fassbender recounts that when he decided to run for Langley City Council in 2001, Palmer knew it was time for his partner to move on and organized a handsome buyout. "Frank was always a straight shooter, and he never forgot the people who had helped his career," he says. "One of my great pleasures during my time at Palmer Jarvis was watching him repeatedly give the shirt off his back to help someone. And he gave without ever expecting anything in return.

"I remember one time telling him, 'Frank, we're having fun and this is a great place to work, but I also really like you as a person.' He was quite taken aback. He didn't know how to respond, because his entire focus had been to make sure others were happy and taken care of."

"Well done is better than well said."
—Benjamin Franklin

I love that quote. Doing something well is better than just saying something well. We've all heard the phrases: actions speak louder than just words; playing a good game is better than talking a good game.

How many detailed business reports or five-year action plans have ever been followed or completed?

Business changes so fast today that an action plan for a year is most likely all that's required. I know we need a plan to get somewhere, but the majority of companies spend too much time creating plans and not enough time following them.

Business is pretty simple: the more clients you have, the healthier it is. You can add employees and costs when you gain more clients, and when you lose clients you reduce these costs. And if things don't work out as well as planned, you change tactics.

Confucius was right when he said that life is simple but we make it complicated. Writing theoretical business plans and reports instead of acting is a good example of that.

Taking action gets results; being passive is losing. Every day, hundreds or even thousands of great ideas are buried and lost because most people are afraid to act upon them. "I could have" or "I should have" is going to get you nowhere.

—FRANK PALMER

Laurel and Hardy

Palmer Jarvis is what made Palmer a local icon, to the extent that the partnership between him and George Jarvis is still discussed at other agencies to this day. In fact, many businesspeople across Canada still refer to Palmer's agency as Palmer Jarvis, or "P.J.", despite DDB's powerhouse brand.

The partnership had begun unremarkably in 1972 when three newcomers joined Simons and Palmer's Trend. The three were Linden Grove, highly regarded for his creative writing talents; Robin Lecky; and George Jarvis, who had made a living as a salesman of airtime at CHQM.

Two years later, Rich Simons left the company and so did Lecky, the latter to become business manager for Griffiths Gibson; Trend was rebranded as Palmer & Jarvis, and a local legend was born.

Palmer says, "George and I quickly became likened to famous comedy teams such as Abbott and Costello, Rowan and Martin, and so forth. But the team we were most commonly identified with was Laurel and Hardy, and that really stuck. In fact, it's stuck to this day, even though the partnership dissolved decades ago. I was the more extroverted half of the duo, and Jarvis was laid-back and easy-going. On a professional level, I was more creative and responsible for delivering the final product, while his great strength was sales and strategy."

The Palmer Jarvis partnership thrived at a time when Vancouver finally became a recognizable international brand due largely to Expo 86, which was staged during the city's one-hundredth anniversary and attracted over twenty-one million visitors from around the globe.

In the 1980s local celebrities gained international attention too: Terry Fox for his attempt to run across Canada; Rick Hansen for his around-the-world Man in Motion tour; and former Tomahawk Restaurant dishwasher Bryan Adams for his music. On the business front, the Port of Vancouver was handling more imports and exports than any other port in North America, and with the opening of Cannell Studios in North Vancouver in 1989, Vancouver became North America's third-largest film production centre after Los Angeles and New York.

The suburban population that was the target of so many Palmer Jarvis ad campaigns had grown to the point where by 1981 it accounted for two-thirds of Greater Vancouver's total population. To accommodate the population's retail needs, Woodward's became the first major Vancouver department store to open on Sundays, and journeying to venues such as Woodward's became easier than ever due to the inauguration of the city's first light rapid transit system, SkyTrain.

There was still a very real sense that Vancouver continued to play catch-up with other urban centres, specifically Toronto. But for many city lovers, Toronto didn't truly become vibrant until it welcomed a mass exodus of people from Montreal in the late 1970s and early 1980s.

Although today Palmer has the time and inclination to elaborate on his fifteen-year partnership with George Jarvis, he finds it difficult to describe the particulars of all the fun and hard work.

He makes an attempt by explaining the differences between him and his ex-partner. "George and I had radically different personalities, but we could make each other laugh and we grew to the point where we would finish each other's sentences," he says. "The Laurel and Hardy reference has been mentioned a lot over the years, and we did indeed think of ourselves as a classic team: Laurel and Hardy, Hope and Crosby, Martin and Lewis, Rowan and Martin. Any of those would apply. That's how we were viewed by our clients, the media, and the business community—two different people who worked together incredibly well."

Like many of the aforementioned celebrity teams, Palmer and Jarvis rarely spent time together after hours. Diplomatically, Palmer concedes that "George appreciated family values way more than I did at the time. He was a devoted family man, whereas I was a workaholic."

But the duo's differences worked to the agency's benefit; Palmer's unquenchable thirst for good times seemed to fuel his ferocious capacity for work, and vice versa, and the flow of ad

campaigns steadily intensified. Jarvis, meanwhile, relished working behind the scenes, quietly ensuring that clients' needs were
taken care of.

Jarvis created a deep level of trust between the agency and its
clients. "He was a real people person who had a knack for gaining
someone's confidence early on, and he never betrayed this confidence, not once," says Palmer. "Also, he was a very careful listener,
much more than me, and this contributed to his trustworthiness."

The thoughtful, straitlaced Jarvis wasn't without his idiosyn-
crasies; he tended to walk about the agency headquarters with
a broken golf club clutched in his hand. "Plus, he would never
come into my office and simply sit on my couch," says Palmer.
"Instead, he would flop onto it and start unloading, as if I were
his psychiatrist."

Now a Vancouver Island resident who visits the mainland
infrequently, Jarvis is reluctant to share his thoughts about the
partnership with outsiders—not because the thoughts are unpleasant, but because he shuns the spotlight. "I never craved attention," he says. "As the second half of the Palmer Jarvis team I had
a high profile in town, but that never really interested me. As far
as I was concerned, I was an anonymous agent acting on behalf
of my clients."

Jarvis, who was born in London, Ontario, and is a year younger than Palmer, got into the packaged goods business as a youth
and moved out west in the late 1960s, where he soon joined CHQM.
"I loved the job from the start," he says. "QM was the businessman's
station, very upper class, and I was surrounded by bright, creative
people. Plus, Vancouver was a small enough town that I was able
to get to know virtually anybody I wanted to, work-wise, and that
included the people in the ad agencies."

Jarvis confesses he was initially better acquainted with Simons and Lecky than Frank Palmer. "I was a salesman, so it was natural that I knew Rich, who was more or less the overseer of the agency, and Robin Lecky, who was extremely well connected with other movers and shakers in Vancouver. Frank was the backroom man who ran the operations side of the business and got the ads and the art done."

Jarvis's defection to the ad agency was remarkably similar to Palmer's. "When Robin decided to leave the company, he asked me if I wanted to buy into it, and I didn't hesitate," he recalls. "To me, it was an unbelievable opportunity to co-own a business."

When Simons left the company, Jarvis became the overall business generator, and Palmer remained the creative force. "It was as simple as that," says Jarvis. "And it turned out to be a magical relationship, very much a Laurel and Hardy partnership as has been repeatedly described."

Self-deprecating to a fault, Jarvis insists more than once that "in the long run my contributions to Palmer Jarvis were small, but I like to think I brought in way more than I ever took out, plus I supported Frank to the end."

Several enduring principles gave Palmer Jarvis its edge, but one of them is so important to Palmer that he discusses it in the form of a story involving hot dogs. In fact, he has told the story so often that some people suspect (incorrectly) it's a tall tale, but that doesn't prevent him from repeating it gleefully, even to those who have heard it just weeks before. "I love telling the hot-dog story because it encapsulates why we distinguished ourselves from the competition, and even though it's pretty simple and maybe lacking in drama, the underlying message is more important today than ever," he says.

The story begins with Palmer soliciting new business and the potential client asking him what makes his company better than other agencies. Without hesitating he replies, "I will always take care of the hot dogs."

The client's eyebrows rise in surprise, and he tells Palmer that recently he'd opened a new store and had invited people to come down and see it. "I told them there would be drinks and hot dogs, but on opening day there were none, and when I got on the phone to complain to our advertising agency they said, 'We don't do hot dogs—but here's the name of a store where you can get them.'"

Palmer finishes the story. "The guy looked at me and said, 'You promise me that you do hot dogs?' and I replied, 'Yes.' The point being, of course, that taking care of the hot dogs means I will always take care of the details."

Although landing an account is an adrenaline rush for Palmer, he is even more addicted to handling its details, no matter how seemingly trivial. "That's where others make mistakes," he says. "Often you'll see huge campaigns developed on a client's behalf, only to have them collapse because someone hadn't paid attention to something they considered trivial but turned out to be of utmost importance to the client."

Another story Palmer tells concerns driving to work daily, and as with the hot-dog story, he uses it to explain Palmer Jarvis's competitive edge. "Some people take the same route to work every day, never deviating, and that has always bothered me because you never find out what's going on beyond your chosen route," he says. "I was very conscious of this during the Palmer Jarvis years: I like to think we were street smart and always drove a different route. It provided us with a constant flow of new information, which in turn gave us great ideas."

The one thing Palmer Jarvis shared with other ad agencies of the era was the penchant of its creative talent to blow off steam from time to time—and Palmer and his crew did so with great relish. On one occasion, while they were staying at a hotel out of town, a morning meeting was scheduled at the hotel's conference room. A stickler for punctuality, Palmer was incensed that the only person who had not shown up for the meeting on time was colleague Mike Tate. So Palmer hurried down the corridor to Tate's guest suite, pounded on his door, informed him that everyone was waiting and stalked back to the conference room.

Peeved at being rushed, Tate decided it would be a good idea to show up at the meeting stark naked. The corridor was deserted, so he removed his clothes, pointedly left his door unlocked, crossed the length of the hallway to the conference room and bid his colleagues a hearty good morning.

Palmer, who was standing unseen in a niche of the room, wasn't about to be upstaged. He ducked through a side exit, hurried down another corridor to Tate's suite, locked his door and returned to the meeting. Tate, having made the impact he had wanted, strolled back to his suite, gripped the door handle—and found it immobile.

Meanwhile, Palmer had closed and locked both conference room doors. "Tate was stuck in the hallway, and within seconds he had scuttled back to the conference room and was pounding on our doors because an elderly couple had emerged from the elevator and was walking toward him," Palmer says. "When we finally let him in, he had the indentations of the door on his chest from pressing up against it so desperately."

*　　*　　*

One of Palmer Jarvis's early accounts was Hudson's Bay, for which the agency supplied all of the venerable retail chain's advertising on the West Coast. Barry Agnew was the Bay's senior vice president of marketing, and his typical method of setting up a business meeting would be to get Palmer on the phone, usually at sunset: "Frank? Barry. Hotel Georgia. You're buying."

Palmer says, "Barry and I would meet for cocktails as often as three nights a week, and it got to the point where if I told my wife 'Barry called,' she would know I would be home late. Barry liked vodka and I liked Scotch, and as long as you did good work for him he was loyal to you."

Years later, when Agnew became national sales director and moved to Toronto, Palmer Jarvis was given the chance to acquire the company's accounts in Calgary, Edmonton and Winnipeg. For Palmer Jarvis to obtain these accounts, Hudson's Bay required it to have a local presence in each of those cities, but Palmer was reluctant to use his own money to set up satellite offices.

However, the idea of expanding Palmer Jarvis across Western Canada was irresistible to Palmer, so he worked out a formula that to this day he believes is the ideal method for developing a national presence. "I went to each city and looked for an agency that had revenues of $2 million or so annually, that understood retail and whose people had a strong work ethic," he explains. "The deal I proposed was that in exchange for me getting equity in these agencies, they would get the Hudson's Bay account. And it worked like a dream. In Calgary we established Freeman Yip Palmer Jarvis, in Edmonton we had Leggatt Palmer Jarvis and in Winnipeg we created Palmer Jarvis RMPR."

When asked if it wouldn't have been preferable to have total control by establishing his own offices, Palmer smiles. "I eventually got that anyway, by taking the fifty-fifty ownerships, converting our equities and creating a new share structure that enabled everyone in the agencies to own a piece of the business, with me as the controlling partner with a 55 per cent share."

This occurred in 1995, at a time when employee ownership was still not common in the Western Canadian business world. "I wasn't trying to play a psychological game the way some company chiefs do whose employees are led to believe they have a say in the direction of business just because they have a fraction of a per cent ownership," says Palmer. "I was simply trying to create an open and honest structure that worked. And it did."

Just as Palmer becomes galvanized when he plots a new joke to play on friends, he's animated in his recollection of how he established a Western Canadian presence. What he discloses next would probably surprise younger folk who revere him as an advertising genius, someone who sweats into the small hours of the morning devising cutting-edge campaigns: "I really enjoy putting business deals together. In fact, to this day it's my most enjoyable part of being in the ad industry. I don't want to give the impression that creating advertising is boring, but there's something about creating deals, or building a company or expanding into different places that makes me profoundly excited."

Building the business in this fashion also enabled Palmer to acquire projects that would otherwise have amounted to client conflict. "A dozen or so years ago, the Labatt account came up for grabs, but we couldn't touch it because we were already handling another beer brand," says Palmer. "At any rate, I called David

Kincaid, the marketing director of Labatt, and asked him what he was looking for in an agency, and he replied, 'The agency that previously represented us was the best, and if you could duplicate that experience we would be ecstatic.'

"The agency in question had merged with another firm, hence the Labatt account going up for grabs. So I called the president of the merged agency, Liz Torley, and said, 'I know you're going to be letting people go, and if that's the case, can we talk about me acquiring them and forming a new team?' She was agreeable, so I flew to Toronto and talked to fifteen people over the course of ten days. Ultimately I convinced about three-quarters of them to come work for me under a new division.

"This was how Downtown Partners was formed and how we got the Labatt account. More importantly in the long run, Downtown enjoyed great success for about eight years, and when it folded most of the talent went on to other things."

Palmer leans forward in his chair for emphasis. "This is why I like strategizing and making deals. Great things happen that benefit a lot of people. Nobody else in the industry was doing these kinds of deals."

For the record, the comet that was Downtown Partners burned brightly during its brief life. Created in 2001, it served a number of other clients including the Red Cross and Anheuser-Busch. The staff, which ultimately swelled to forty people, also achieved the distinction of presiding over the only Canadian agency ever to create ads that ran during US broadcasts of the Super Bowl; in fact, USA Today deemed the Anheuser-Busch ads among the most popular in America during the 2003 Super Bowl broadcast.

Downtown's success continued in its sophomore year at the 2002 Cannes Lions International Festival of Creativity, when it be-

Frank, age six, on a Shetland pony—no doubt considering an early franchise opportunity in the equine world with a price increase to twenty-five cents per ride.

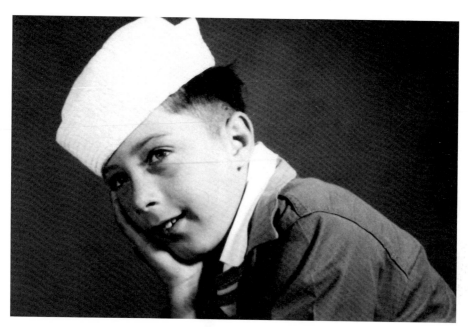

Frank, age seven, posing in a sailor boy hat; it was around this time he was getting picked last for sports teams and determining ways to do his own picking in life.

Frank's first car, a 1947 Mercury two-door, being customized circa 1960: an early example of his passion for creating things that looked different.

Actor Lorne Greene and Frank Palmer pose on Seymour Mountain in North Vancouver, BC, circa 1978. The two became fast friends after Palmer retained Greene to appear in a series of Bank of British Columbia television ads.

Ron Woodall and Frank Palmer holding the new Palmer Jarvis logo sign, circa 1990, to announce Ron joining the team as the new executive creative director.

Vancouver and Victoria Palmer Jarvis DDB senior management retreat—a regular event that involved paintball shootouts to get everyone fired up for work in the coming year.

Frank and Frank's face on a sumo-wrestler cut-out—a staff gag circa 1992.
Gags like this were a common occurrence at Palmer Jarvis.

Palmer Jarvis partners and shareholders pose for a group photo after selling the company to DDB Worldwide, a division of Omnicom, in 1997. Frank Palmer stands fourth from the left in the back row.

Having fun with "Whazzup" beer during the Anheuser-Busch account in 1999. Left to right: Tony Alitilia, President and CEO of Downtown Partners; Keith Reinhard, Chairman Emeritus of DDB Worldwide; Frank Palmer, President of DDB Canada.

Frank wins the 1999 Ernst & Young Entrepreneur of the Year Award.

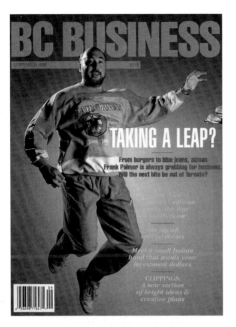

Cover of the September 1989 issue, courtesy of *BCBusiness* magazine.

Cover of the August 2008 issue, courtesy of *Strategy* magazine.

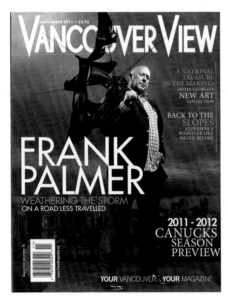

Cover of the November 2011 issue, courtesy of *Vancouver View* magazine.

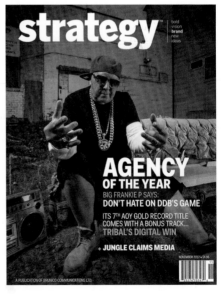

Cover of the November 2012 issue, courtesy of *Strategy* magazine.

Frank sits in the Big Idea Chair after speaking at Yahoo in 2004 about "Why Creative Is Important"—an ongoing theme of his public speeches.

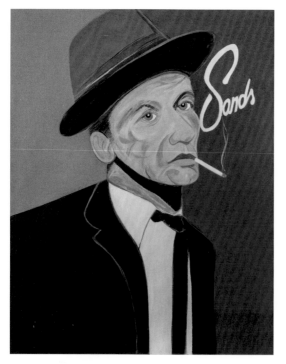

Frank's 2017 painting, *Frank Sinatra* (acrylic on canvas), hangs in his Palm Springs home. As a lifelong fan of the crooner, Frank hopes to have Sinatra's rendition of "My Way" played at his funeral; it sums up his approach to both life and business.

came the only Canadian agency to win in the TV category ("Fridge," created for Anheuser-Busch, received a Gold Lion); meanwhile, its K-tel parody "Ulterior Emotions" for Labatt Breweries received a Silver Lion in the film category.

In 2003 Downtown scored big again, becoming the only Canadian agency to win the Cannes TV Gold, for "History" and "Greeting Cards." Other accolades would follow.

Still, Labatt represented nearly 40 per cent of Downtown's revenues, and when the relationship ended in 2007, industry pundits speculated that the boutique agency was struggling. When Downtown announced it was closing its doors in 2008, Philippe Garneau, executive creative director of GWP Brand Engineering, which is based in Toronto, told the press that no owner wants to be overly dependent on a single client, and although he agreed that launching an agency brand around a major account is a great base, he warned that such an account could become too dominant in the agency's development.

* * *

A deal of a different sort cemented Palmer Jarvis's status as a force with which to be reckoned in Western Canada. "George's people skills and the trust he established with clients were a huge factor in our winning the McDonald's account for all of British Columbia in 1973," says Palmer. Notorious for being tough-as-nails businesspeople, the policy makers at McDonald's carefully assessed the pitches of different ad agencies, including Palmer Jarvis, before phoning Palmer to say they would be visiting his office to ask a few more "tough questions" about their approach to marketing.

Palmer recalls, "We were already nervous as hell and didn't know what else we could possibly do to win the account, so this was the last thing we wanted to hear. We sweated bullets waiting for them to arrive, and when they did they were carrying hamburgers, milkshakes and french fries—congratulations for us being the winning agency. The relief we felt was palpable."

Dean Mailey worked for *Vancouver Sun* newspaper columnist Jack Wasserman during this time. "As soon as Frank and George landed the McDonald's account, they strutted into Jack's office and told him he should write about it in his column," he says. "I know George was low-key, but they both had a knack for getting their agency as much media exposure as possible."

Palmer describes McDonald's as "a very complex, demanding account. Common sense dictated that you had to become friends with the owner/operators, as well as the people in the Western Canada head office and the national head office—and once again George was the person who nurtured these relationships."

Jarvis remarks, "Establishing relations with the McDonald's people was easy because from the owner/operators all the way up to McDonald's Canada executive vice president Ron Marcoux, I really loved these people. Also, there was a palpable sense of building something new across Canada that was exciting to be a part of."

Jarvis views McDonald's as the epitome of what he wanted to accomplish when he joined Simons Palmer and Lecky. "As Red Robinson points out, ad agencies wanted nothing to do with chain retailers, who had unbelievably cheap lineage rates with the local newspapers that nobody knew how to overcome. During this time radio and television stations were only beginning to focus on chain retail; they got into it because they established a rate and paid a commission to the agencies. In other words, deals were being made whereby retailers were booked into newspapers for a great price on the understanding that radio and TV also got a portion of the deal.

"Agencies had absolutely no idea how to make money from retail under these circumstances, but the fact was they simply didn't understand the chain retail business. Having worked in sales at CHQM, I had quite a lot of experience. So, incidentally, did Robin Lecky, his father having been a manager at *The Vancouver Sun* and his mother a retail worker.

"In any event, that's why I was so passionate about developing close relations with McDonald's—that and the fact it's a first-class organization. With our focus on service we provided everything from the design and printing of their coupons to television ads, something most agencies would never do."

Before long, Palmer and Jarvis's skill in opening new McDonald's restaurants in BC, supervising their public relations campaigns and organizing charity fundraisers compelled them to go after other McDonald's accounts in Western Canada. "We pitched the company in each of the cities where we had offices and wound up winning them all," says Palmer proudly.

Jim Peacock, president of Peacock Public Relations in Vancouver, expressed his admiration for Palmer's limitless drive to the press in 1994, pointing out that Palmer was thinking of new ideas not only during formal brainstorming sessions but while on the road with Ron Marcoux. Peacock also noted that many of Palmer's ideas were focused on fulfilling community needs on behalf of the hamburger giant.

Rivals, however, were less enthusiastic about Palmer's business conduct. "I already mentioned how he pissed off other agencies by constantly trying to steal their accounts, and in an industry that is notorious for being cutthroat, Frank led the pack," says Bob Bryant. "We became friends after I retired in 2004, but when I was running Bryant, Fulton & Shee, my opinion was that if you shook hands with Frank, you'd be wise to count your fingers afterward. In fact, we weren't so much rivals as we were enemies."

Bryant, who started his career by joining Foster Advertising in 1965, was frequently bewildered by the stunts Palmer pulled in his attempt to win accounts. "One of the very few times we won an account and Frank didn't was the time we obtained BC Lottery Corporation as a client," he recalls. "After the fact a BC Lottery representative told us that when the decision makers were preparing to review the proposals, they were warned not to fall for any tricks. And she said, 'Thank God they didn't, because Frank came in and just before he made his pitch he told everyone, "I want you to know we want your business, and if we get it we'll be with you 100 per cent."

According to Bryant, Palmer then led everyone outside into the parking lot, where they found a bus festooned with Palmer Jarvis banners and with all of the Palmer Jarvis staff on board.

On another occasion, a hospital that had shortlisted a group of agencies telephoned Bryant for advice, and Bryant soon learned that Palmer Jarvis was not on the shortlist. "The hospital representative told me that she had phoned Frank to give him the bad news, and Frank replied, 'That's okay, but we've done a whole bunch of work on your project anyway, so let me come in and I'll pitch it to you for free.' That's quintessential Frank; he simply couldn't take no for an answer."

Palmer insists that some of the "value added" services he provided during pitches were entirely in keeping with his company's business philosophy. "We once pitched to Playland and the Pacific National Exhibition at seven o'clock at night, and because we were the seventh to pitch and the previous pitches had each been about a half hour long, I knew nobody had yet had dinner," he recalls. "So I made sure to bring in a Mr. Tube Steak, and when I made my pitch I said something along the lines of, 'Look, I appreciate that you must be tired and hungry at this point, so let's dig in'—and we served them hot dogs right there and then."

Even the more outrageous tales involving Palmer that are probably urban myths seem to ring true. "Palmer Jarvis and my agency were fighting to get the Woodward's account, and we lost because we screwed up our pitch: during a crucial moment in his presentation, Darrel Shee completely forgot 'Chunky' Woodward's name and stood there for what seemed like an eternity before referring to him as 'Woodbin,'" Bryant says. "Anyway, I heard later on that during the culmination of his pitch, Frank got out of his chair, climbed up on the boardroom table, laid down on it and declared, 'I'm not leaving until you give us the account.'"

Laughing, Bryant admits the story may well be apocryphal. "But if it were true, it wouldn't surprise me a bit."

Not surprisingly, Palmer derives a good deal of amusement from these anecdotes. He is eager to add, though, that the showmanship was always informed by voluminous research. "I was bullish about getting the Save-On-Foods account some years ago, but it was a conflict of interest because we had Safeway," he says. "However, when I found out that Safeway was going to pull all of its accounts in Canada and take them to San Francisco, I got on the phone to Brian Piwek, president of the Overwaitea Food Group and owner of Save-On, and explained what was about to happen. He was in an awkward spot, because he'd already been in talks with five other agencies for about a month. I stressed that we had lots of grocery experience and knew the language.

"Piwek told me, 'You'll be coming in from behind,' but he finally agreed to meet with me, in private. So we met in a room I'd booked at the Hotel Vancouver, and the upshot was he agreed to allow us to pitch and supplied us the same brief he'd given the other agencies. From that point on, we knocked ourselves out and worked around the clock to determine exactly what each Save-On-Foods department wanted and needed. We learned what was of paramount importance to the company overall, and when we finally made our presentation we were able to propose how to improve their flyers, suggested new signage and described television spots. We blew everyone else out of the water, and for the next five years Save-On-Foods was our favourite client."

Palmer concludes, "I'm no stranger to razzle-dazzle. But it's never empty pyrotechnics. It's always supported by plenty of homework, to the point where we can converse easily in the client's language."

* * *

Palmer strongly believes that the more hands-on research that is conducted about a client's product, the better the campaign becomes. Sometimes, investigative reporting is responsible for an entire campaign coming to life. "We were tasked at one point to market vitamins," he recalls. "It turned out to be a nightmare, because with the thousands of vitamins and minerals glutting the market, we couldn't figure out how these ones were any different from the others, no matter how hard we tried."

In desperation, Palmer and his colleagues finally paid a visit to the plant where the vitamins were manufactured. As he watched with glazed eyes the intricate and repetitive processes that went into formulating, bottling and packaging the pills, Palmer overheard a worker tell one of his team members, "We manufacture our pills without alcohol."

Palmer explains, "Back then alcohol was widely used as a binding agent in the formulation of vitamins. And when I heard that comment, bingo, we had our ad campaign."

Such diligence came at a cost, at least as far as others were concerned. "The way I viewed the Palmer Jarvis partnership was that George seemed to love life, but despite his antics Frank was unusually focused on work, almost to the point where he had blinders on," says Brian Robertson.

Palmer becomes awkward when asked to describe his home life. "I'm not the best family man. I'll admit that, and obviously I'm not great at marriage. But it wasn't as if I didn't care about my wife or kids. Although I'd like to think that nothing in life is really planned, Kathy and I deliberately planned to have children, and when my son and daughter were born five years apart from each other, my first feeling was a tremendous sense of obligation to take care of them. To me, that meant making damned sure my agency kept growing."

After further awkward introspection, Palmer adds, "But I was also very aware that my dad had hated his job at the bakery. He couldn't stand any of it, even though it was of his own doing. I wasn't going to have a life like that. I loved the business I was in and I loved having fun in it, and nothing was going to make me deviate from my behaviour."

Hilary Robertson notes that Palmer's son, Darren, exhibits a lot of his father's traits. "He's now a family man with two kids, and no matter what he does, he feels compelled to do it perfectly. He's an extremely hard and conscientious worker, and it drives him crazy if he can't live up to his own high standards."

Hugh Ruthven says, "Frank's relentless pursuit of business has obviously been at the expense of his personal relationships, specifically his kids. It's the one aspect of his life that has proven to be a huge imbalance, and I strongly suspect he would do things differently if given a second chance."

To which Marika adds cryptically, "His private life has not been easy in this respect."

Palmer's singular focus on hard work and growth made Palmer Jarvis a force to be reckoned with, and success enabled him to not only take care of his family financially, but also give younger colleagues a leg up in the industry. Dean Mailey says, "In 1981 I opened my own agency and did well until the economy took a nose dive, so I went to Palmer Jarvis hoping they would provide me with financing in exchange for services. As it turned out, Frank was looking for an agency that could handle business that would have otherwise conflicted with his existing accounts, and he viewed me as the ideal candidate."

Mailey recalls the circumstances of that meeting. "Frank and George owned a building on Hornby Street, and their offices on the third floor were a block long. Initially I stated my case to Frank, and when George wandered by Frank called out, 'Hey George, I need a cheque from you.' The transaction was as casual as that, even though it meant the world to me in terms of solidifying my career."

Although many colleagues such as Chris Staples testify that Palmer's true greatness lies in business management (something that has been woefully downplayed by the media in favour of depicting Palmer as a creative genius), Mailey believes Palmer's skills as an artist haven't yet been given their proper due. "I saw them for myself one evening in 1983 in Frank's Point Grey townhouse," he says. "We were talking about how to present art while pitching ad campaigns; this was back when you presented renderings on boards, not like today when the art is completed right down to a T. Anyway, Frank took out his sketchpad and began sketching, and his technique was amazing. Years later he began showing me his personal artwork: very modernistic, bold, geometric designs that blew me away. So yes, Frank is a visualist, perfectly suited for the ad world that existed at the point he entered it."

Palmer as a visualist may also explain other character traits. "I always found it peculiar that after Frank's second marriage fell apart and before he finally met Marika, the discrepancy between the women he was attracted to professionally and personally was huge," says Hilary Robertson. "In business, he was—and still is—drawn to smart, powerful women. He admired and trusted them far more than he did men. Yet during the years he was a man about town, the women he chose were completely different: all flash, all glitz. And it struck me that being such a visualist by nature, a lot of Frank's values were based on appearance."

Marika bursts out laughing at the description of Palmer the visualist. "That's an understatement if applied to the past women in his life," she says. "He was like a compass that spun in all directions. When he first met my mother he couldn't take his eyes off her, to the point where it drove her up the wall."

It's not surprising, then, that Palmer especially enjoyed organizing projects in the most visual of mediums, television commercials, which also gave him the opportunity to rub shoulders with old-time Hollywood stars. One of the first celebrities to cross his path was Lyon Hyman Green, better known to the world as Lorne Greene, "The Voice of Doom" to Canada's World War II radio audiences and Ben Cartwright of *Bonanza* fame.

Palmer retained Greene, just after the demise of *Bonanza*, to appear in a series of Bank of British Columbia television ads. "Our goal was to demonstrate to viewers that the bank wasn't just a local business," says Palmer. "Greene received $25,000 for each of the three TV spots, and they were a huge success; that was the beginning of a three-year relationship with Greene, by the end of which he was getting over $100,000 for each spot."

Palmer and Greene became friends, and Palmer was amused by the star's eccentricities. "He was a pill freak, meaning vitamin pills. He was concerned about his health, and I never saw so many vitamin bottles as I did when I would pick him up at his suite in the Bayshore Inn."

Greene, a formidable man obsessed with image, also had the habit of telling people he was six foot one when in fact he was five foot ten. "We had a photo taken of us standing together on Cypress Mountain, and Greene made me stand in a hole so it would look like he was taller than me," Palmer recalls.

But what impressed Palmer the most about Greene was his timing. "He would be in a studio and do a reading, and at the end of the reading he would say, 'That was fifty-three seconds, right?' We would look at our stopwatches, and sure as hell it was fifty-three seconds on the nose. It was uncanny."

Palmer also masterminded a series of television commercials with Raymond Burr and was equally impressed by the actor's technical skills. "He was a very demanding individual, but he always knew his lines and even more so knew when a take was the one to print. Sometimes the director would say, 'Let's do one more take for safety,' and Burr would reply, 'No, we've got it, let's move on.' And he always turned out to be right."

Leslie Nielsen was yet another old-school Hollywood celebrity whose professionalism impressed Palmer, although the first time they met Palmer was somewhat bewildered by the star's physical condition. "When we shook hands upon meeting each other for the first time, he let out a fart," Palmer recalls. "I didn't want to say anything, because the guy was getting up in age and we all accidentally let one go now and then. But when we sat down, he let out another fart, and I tried like hell to pretend I hadn't heard it. A minute went by and then he really let one rip, and it must have been the look on my face because he suddenly cracked up and took his hand out of his pocket; he was holding a bladder that made the fart noises."

*   *   *

The recollection of any business loss or shortcoming, no matter how far in the past, causes Palmer's face to contort worriedly. Rivalries he can understand, people not liking him he can shrug off, but whenever he's reminded of a job not done to a client's satisfaction, his playfulness evaporates and is replaced by irritation. Palmer becomes especially irritated when discussing how he lost the Edmonton McDonald's account (which, like the Juan Valdez incident years later, occurred after George Jarvis had left the business).

As Palmer tells it, "We had been running into difficulties in that city, and the perception was we simply weren't doing a good enough job. I'll never forget the day the axe fell. I was making a presentation to a group of McDonald's upper management, including my biggest boss, Ron Marcoux. Even as I was talking I knew beyond a doubt that it wasn't going well, and at one point Marcoux was handed a slip of paper, which he read, tore up and pushed into a coffee cup."

Shaking his head at the still-vivid image, Palmer continues. "When the presentation was over everyone left for a break, so I took the pieces of paper from the cup and put them back together. The note read, 'Time for an agency review.' It wasn't a big surprise, but those words were an icy shock nonetheless. And sure as hell, we lost Edmonton."

Even though there's a happy ending to the story, it doesn't give Palmer much cheer. "A few years later, Marcoux and his colleagues decided to give us back Edmonton because we had privately resolved to not repeat the debacle and simply go full steam in the other cities. Our tenacity impressed them, plus I suspect they weren't so happy with the agency that replaced us."

Palmer's gloom fills his office like smog. He even has trouble making eye contact. "To this day, the memory of losing Edmonton scares the hell out of me. We may have got it back because we worked our asses off to keep the rest of the McDonald's business, but the sticking point for me is that we lost it to begin with. Even though the Juan Valdez incident was far more devastating in terms of lost revenue and the fact we had to lay off people, it was due to politics. The Edmonton loss was due to us being perceived as delivering less-than-excellent work."

For people who make a living producing words or images, the toughest thing to face is that even the most carefully thought-out product can fall flat depending on the mood of the people it's pitched to. This subjectivity is especially tough on the psyches of those who crave control like Palmer, and it's enough to turn the toughest practitioners to drink. Developing a knack for shrugging off losses and moving on to the next assignment is an enviable asset.

Palmer has always been able to move on to the next assignment, but he's never been able to shrug off a loss. The Edmonton story compels him to reveal a side of his personality few outsiders are privy to. "I'm plagued by the notion that I'm only a few wrong moves away from living in a cardboard box under a bridge," he says. "I felt that way working as a kid in the bakery, and no amount of success since then has changed me. Everything I've worked for could be lost if I went off my game, even temporarily." Fear as much as curiosity has been Palmer's lifelong muse, and the passage of time has only made it more acute.

Still, Palmer has nothing but admiration for McDonald's. "It's one of these accounts you never get out of your blood."

He also credits the organization for having an exceptional sense of humour. The most expensive joke Palmer ever pulled was on Peter Beresford, McDonald's senior vice president of worldwide marketing. When the Commonwealth Games were scheduled to take place in Victoria in 1994, Beresford made the mistake of telling Palmer, a diehard patriot, that he didn't want to be a sponsor.

Upset that a good marketing opportunity was about to go down the drain, Palmer hired a Vancouver *Globe and Mail* reporter to interview Beresford about his thoughts on the Commonwealth Games and his reluctance to sponsor them. "Peter made all sorts of diplomatic remarks, but none of them mattered because the reporter went back to the newsroom and cranked out a column about how Peter thought Victoria was a dead zone and a pissy little city," he recalls. "I then paid *The Globe and Mail* to print two hundred copies of the next day's edition with the column and its horrific phony quotes on the front page of the business section. This was for the benefit of two hundred McDonald's franchise owner/operators who just happened to be in town from across Canada. I went to the hotel they were staying at and quietly slipped a copy of the paper under their doors."

When the owner/operators woke up and read the bogus interview, they thought Beresford had taken leave of his senses and quickly confronted him. Alarmed, Beresford grabbed a copy of the paper, read the column and almost keeled over. Palmer says, "He said, 'I never said any of this!' and phoned *The Globe and Mail* business editor. 'What are you doing to me with this story?' he yelled, and the editor replied, 'What the hell are you talking about?' and at that point Peter realized he'd been had. He had a good laugh—and McDonald's ultimately sponsored the games."

"It pays to be nice to the people you meet on the way up, for they are the same people you meet on the way down."

—Walter Winchell

I'm sure all of you have heard that famous saying before? Legendary newspaper columnist Walter Winchell gets credit for it, but a number of other folk lay claim to it too. If you haven't come across it before, it's worth remembering and more importantly putting into practice.

Far too many people I've come across in business have, upon achieving success, become very important in their own mind. These bores fully believe they are better than you and me and that any success they enjoy is 100 per cent due to their own efforts and talent.

In any career, we don't usually get to the top of our game without lots of help from others. Each and every step to success is due not only to your efforts and talent, but also to the assistance of people who want you to succeed. If you think about your growth as a ladder to success, try to remember that even if you reach the top rung, no one stays on top forever. And that as you come down, you will be placing your feet on the same steps that the people you met going up are holding onto.

If you treated those who helped you on the way up poorly, some of them will do their best to not help you on your way down. In fact, they will probably go out of their way to trip you.

If you were kind and respectful to them on your career rise, they will treat you with kindness and respect on the way down.

— FRANK PALMER

The Split

Palmer and Jarvis used to meet weekly at the old Bayshore Inn to discuss past and upcoming events and other points of business. It was a prime location, with unparalleled views of nearby Stanley Park, the floating gas stations in Coal Harbour and the long, tan skyline of North Vancouver, dwarfed by the North Shore Mountains.

After one of these meetings in 1989, as they walked to the parking lot Jarvis informed Palmer that he was leaving the agency to work for McDonald's.

Palmer felt as if he'd been hit by a truck. "I was in shock, and

I guess in my state of shock I wondered why he waited until we were heading for our cars to tell me," he recalls.

Jarvis left when the agency still had the McDonald's account, and by Palmer's own admission, "I worried like hell about what would happen to that account, because it was George who had developed and maintained the relationship; now I would have to step in and attempt to establish the same deep level of trust that he seemed to have earned so casually. In short, I had to ante up my game at a time when I thought my game was at its peak."

The following day, Ron Marcoux phoned Palmer and asked if he had any problems with Jarvis jumping ship. Palmer said no but added that he doubted Jarvis would stay with McDonald's for very long. "I only mentioned that because I knew George so well; he couldn't follow routines, and if there's any business that is defined by its routines, it's McDonald's."

Not much has been written about Palmer having to assume Jarvis's role as ambassador to McDonald's, and Palmer himself dismisses the task with terse comments such as "I just did what needed to be done." It falls upon Hugh Ruthven to elaborate on the unenviable challenge: "George Jarvis was a hard act to follow; he was the quintessential relationship man, and the relationships he had established with upper management and the licensees were genuine, complex, mutually fulfilling—in short, the result of years of hard work," he says. "I'm sure Frank must have been terrified. In fact, I know that he was initially terrified of Ron Marcoux."

But instead of letting his fear get the better of him, Palmer immediately committed to finding out everything about McDonald's and the individuals who ran the organization. "He did a lot of footwork, a lot of homework, and pretty soon he was filling the void left by George," says Ruthven. "The McDonald's people responded to his efforts, and of course they liked Frank on a personal level. Frank going the extra mile paid off in the long run too, long after he lost the McDonald's account, because Ron became genuinely interested in his welfare. Ron taught him a lot, helped him elevate his management game."

Marcoux, who was notorious for running an extremely tight ship, was not above matching Palmer's penchant for gags. Ruthven recalls, "One time when Palmer Jarvis and McDonald's agreed that Big Macs should temporarily go on sale for $1.99, Ron quietly instructed several of his restaurants near the Palmer Jarvis headquarters that they would advertise the Big Macs on phony billboards at a ridiculously low price of sixty-nine cents. When the bogus billboards were installed outside the restaurants, he then phoned Frank and screamed, 'What the hell are you doing, trying to bankrupt me?'

"Frank babbled, 'I don't know what you're talking about.' Ron shouted, 'Selling Big Macs at sixty-nine cents—are you out of your mind?' Frank babbled some more, and Ron said, 'If you don't believe me then go outside and see for yourself'—and slammed down the phone. Frank hurried to the nearest McDonald's, saw the sixty-nine-cent billboards and almost had a heart attack."

During these chaotic times, Palmer inadvertently created competition for himself in the form of Bob Stamnes, who joined Palmer Jarvis in 1985, a few years earlier. "I had started out in radio doing everything, even voice work, and then I became a promotions director before getting fired," Stamnes says. "I was twenty-five and still living with my parents, and one morning while recovering from a night of heavy drinking I went to a local fast-food joint and bumped into an old friend, David Dougherty, who was all dressed up and looking extremely debonair, ready to go see a client. We got to talking, and he told me I should see George Jarvis about a job. David's appearance impressed me so much that I did. George subsequently hired me to sell McDonald's coupons, and I thought I'd died and gone to heaven."

Under Jarvis's tutelage Stamnes slowly worked his way up the corporate ladder, never once rubbing shoulders with Palmer until Jarvis decided to leave the agency. "My first interaction with Frank was when he pointed a finger at me and said, 'I want to talk to you,'" says Stamnes. "He wanted me to go to Winnipeg to handle the McDonald's account in that region, at a salary of $40,000 annually. And I went without hesitation, because among many other things it was a chance to be a big fish in a small pond."

Stamnes remembers Winnipeg as "a fantastic two-year experience because the city, isolated as it was from undue market influence, was treated as a testing ground for McDonald's. A lot of exciting things went on as a result. However, it was also in Winnipeg that I decided to open my own agency, with absolutely no money but fortified with a partner and lots of confidence. George Jarvis and Red Robinson gave me encouragement, and when I finally went to Frank about it, he gave me his blessing. He asked, 'If it doesn't work out will you come back and work for me?' And I replied, 'No, because I'll make sure it works out.'"

Stamnes grins like a schoolboy. "I think our friendship began at that moment, because Frank has a deep respect for risk takers."

After relocating in Vancouver, Stamnes and his business partner slept in friends' apartments and got about on foot (with less than $100 in their pockets, they could hardly afford a car). Palmer recalls, "They eventually came to me asking for a partnership, and we went into it fifty-fifty." Stamnes also borrowed $25,000 from his parents, and with these combined resources a new agency was born. "I wound up paying my parents back within a year and sent them on a cruise," Stamnes says.

Glennie Stamnes (later Elevator) garnered glowing press reviews for its work, including ad campaigns for Toyota. "Back then it was easy to differentiate ourselves from the competition," says Stamnes. "In Vancouver there were big agencies and boutiques, but nothing in between such as a company with big-agency experience but that still worked hands-on with clients. Our strategy paid off, because the Palmer Jarvises of the world kept getting bigger, and the boutiques either became big or went out of business or got purchased.

"What also worked was our refusal to take on too much business or clients that didn't fit our world view. People said, 'Who the fuck do these guys think they are?' and it really put us on the map."

As with so many things in the ad world, adversity sometimes became an asset. "For example, my partner and I were both thirty, footloose and fancy-free," says Stamnes. "So footloose, in fact, that we couldn't even get a credit card. So when we began wooing Toyota by taking the executives to lunch, I made sure beforehand to take lots of money out of the bank. The sight of me pulling out a huge wad of bills to settle the tab turned out to be very impressive."

Palmer observed Stamnes's rise with mixed feelings. "Bob remains a close friend, but I think he began to take the press's depiction of him as a creative force too seriously," he says. "I kept thinking, 'My God, I'm the one responsible for this new competition.' Fortunately, nobody in my inner circle knew I was a partner, although eventually the partnership was dissolved when I accepted a modest buyout."

Stamnes credits Palmer for his start as well as for helping him fifteen years ago when his agency teetered on the verge of bankruptcy. "Clients weren't paying, the bottom had dropped out of the dot-com business and I was $1.7 million in debt," he says. "I almost lost my company, but Frank went to my creditors and told them, 'Give Bobby another chance, he's good for the money.' And they did. And I slowly climbed out of the hole."

After a pause, during which he takes in the sunshine spilling into his office beside the iron latticework of the Granville Street Bridge, Stamnes adds, "Frank's demonstration of faith is something I'll never forget."

Stamnes and Palmer have the kind of relationship whereby they can discuss each other's faults without fear of hurting each other's feelings. As a result, Stamnes was at Palmer's side through many phases of his personal and professional life. "I'll never forget when Frank's second marriage broke up. He told me, 'Bobby, she's even taken half the water out of our pool!' But once he got through the divorce, we wound up having a hell of a good time together. We would go on holidays and carouse, which one time culminated in him pouring the red wine into the tub while I was taking a shower," Stamnes recalls. "Goddamn it, I was convinced blood was coming out of my ass."

✳   ✳   ✳

It takes several meetings with Jarvis before he discloses the reasons that led him to leave the agency, and even then he chooses his words carefully. He begins by saying, "The first reason for leaving was that business had become very successful, and I was happy that we'd hit an equilibrium of making money and having fun.

"But on a fundamental level, to me the ad world was all about doing a great job and enjoying client relationships. To Frank, it was all about acquiring more and more control."

Jarvis nods when told about Palmer's disclosure of getting a thrill from opening offices in other cities. "There you go. That's a prime example of something I wasn't interested in, acquiring businesses just for the sake of taking things over. He was forever adding partners, when I figured I was the only partner who should have mattered. In the end, I decided all these partners could buy me out without hurting the business, and since I'd been given a chance to work for McDonald's I finally made the leap."

A story about Palmer turning forty, which occurred nine years before Jarvis left the agency, illustrates how deeply his desire for control is engrained in his psyche. "I had left Kathy and was having a classic midlife crisis when a friend persuaded me to attend a self-help seminar featuring someone called Randy Revell," he recalls. "It was a five-day course, and early on I found myself having to play a musical chairs–type game with the other participants, with pop versions of Beethoven's music playing in the background.

"The whole thing was driving me nuts. Randy noticed this and said to me, 'You're obviously not getting into this.' I replied, 'No, I'm not. I think this whole thing is a scam, starting with your name and that fucking music. I think you're trying to brainwash us.'"

After more games and incremental increases in Palmer's blood pressure, the participants were evaluated according to the behaviour they had demonstrated. "I fell into the category of a 'controller/promoter,' only everyone felt compelled to label me a 'controlling controller/promoter,' and I wound up in a group of other controllers," Palmer says. "To me it was a big joke and a complete waste of time. At one point each group had to stage a play as part of our self-help. I was so sick of the tedium that I didn't want any of the controllers yapping at me, so I threatened to quit unless I staged the play exactly my way." Even in the indulgent arena of adult make-believe, Palmer has to reign supreme.

For the record, Palmer's curiosity about himself and his place in the world has led him to occasionally visit self-help gurus, experiences that are inevitably undone by a growing suspicion that he is being taken advantage of. On one occasion, a local practitioner tried to alleviate several decades' worth of Palmer's baggage by persuading him to thrust his arm out of his office window. The practitioner shook the arm, chanting, "Your arm is getting lighter, lighter. It weighs almost nothing. Do you feel yourself any lighter?" To which Palmer, thoroughly humiliated, replied, "Yes, I feel a whole lot lighter. I went to the bathroom ten minutes ago."

Jarvis stresses there wasn't any blowout that compelled him to leave Palmer, nor were there bad feelings that had been percolating over the years. "I simply couldn't keep up with the pace anymore. Meaning, Frank's pace. Don't get me wrong—Frank is one of a kind, and the world will be poorer without him. I'll never forget the time he purchased a massive Heidelberg press and installed it in the basement of our office; although it operated, we weren't in the printing business! It was purely for show, to add substance to a meeting and show clients we could turn things around very quickly. That was Frank in a nutshell—great showmanship.

"And we did have a lot of fun, no question. At times I made him just as crazy as he made me. It particularly used to bug him that I drove around town in an old beater. He was forever coming over to me saying he had lined up a deal to get me the latest model Cadillac or Oldsmobile or whatever, and when I turned him down the baffled expression on his face was something to behold. Frank was incapable of going through the front door of a showroom without emerging at the back end with a brand new car, and this was one of many quirks that made him so likeable."

After a pause, he says, "But I had a great wife as well as kids in high school, and it had become increasingly tough over the years to juggle my responsibilities to them with being out every night with Frank."

Jarvis had also become increasingly perplexed by Frank's relationship with women. "It's not something that influenced my decision to quit, but it was another thing that demonstrated how different we were. For example, I remember being best man when Frank married his second wife, Laura. My wife and I went to Europe soon after for a vacation, and when we got back Frank was already getting a divorce! It was something that was impossible for me to relate to."

Jarvis is not exaggerating. Palmer conducted an affair with Laura for close to five years before finally marrying her; she left him for a bus driver seven weeks after the wedding. "In retrospect it was five years of hell, because I was still married and I didn't want to hurt my wife or kids but obviously was doing so," Palmer says. "The affair affected other people too, but I went right on doing what I was doing. In some ways I thought marriage would resolve a lot of the problems, and when Laura left I went into a deep funk that lasted months."

The funk was so severe that Palmer let the financial aspect of his company slide. Finally, one morning in his office, his bank manager, John Cooper, and one of the bank's accountants visited him. "Do you know your receivables are ninety to 120 days?" Cooper asked.

"Yep," Palmer replied indifferently.

"Do you know you're running behind on billing your clients?"

"Yep."

"And do you know you have no earnings in your account?"

"Yes, I know that too."

"And no guarantees?"

"Yep."

Cooper cut to the chase. "Well then Frank, you've got forty-eight hours to sign over everything you've got as collateral."

Palmer sat bolt upright in his chair as if ice water had been dashed in his face. His funk was replaced by an even worse sensation of anxiety. If he signed, he would be putting his personal equity on the line on behalf of his agency. If he didn't sign, it would likely spell the end for the company and mean pink slips for about sixty people.

Palmer recalls, "It was as if Cooper had put a gun to my head and was about to pull the trigger. So I signed. And to tell the truth it was the best thing that had ever happened to me, because it woke me up. Not that I enjoyed signing my assets away, by any means."

The recollection of John Cooper's ultimatum causes Palmer to remember another time when he arranged a million-dollar line of credit from the bank on his company's behalf and wound up being on the hook for the entire sum because none of his partners would co-sign the deal. "So what I did was take a 10 per cent fee yearly on that million bucks as compensation," he says. "That really pissed off my partners. 'You can't do that,' they complained. And I said, 'Just watch me. As we speak, my balls are on display in a jar in the showcase window of the bank, so I'm damned well taking 10 per cent. You guys may have skills that advance this company, but you don't have any balls. At least, not in a jar for the entire world to see.'"

Palmer's tumultuous lifestyle notwithstanding, Jarvis has remained a friend. "I hope I was a good partner to him," he says. "I like to think that during our time together I may have also protected him somewhat, because he was generous to a fault. An awful lot of people took his money and didn't give much value in return."

What puzzled Palmer the most about the breakup was Jarvis's assertion that he couldn't keep up with Palmer's pace. "I was mystified by that, because I knew the pressure to keep up would be even greater at McDonald's."

For the record, Jarvis says this of his time at the fast-food giant: "It was a wonderful part of my life that lasted a few years." He ultimately enjoyed a longer-lasting career by becoming one of Vancouver's notable philanthropists.

Palmer concedes that everything Jarvis has said about their partnership is true. "Whenever I was with someone I used to say to myself, 'I'm going to beat you. If you work ten hours a day, I'll work twelve,' and so on. As for women, everyone in this business was a cock hound. At least, most of us were. We all chased women at one point or another, and maybe I was a little more aggressive at it when I was a bachelor."

Palmer summarizes the partnership thus: "The success I've had is due to a lot of people, and George Jarvis is most certainly high on that list. So too is Rich Simons, despite the fact I used to have a recurring dream that I was on trial for murdering him. In this dream the judge asks me, 'Why did you kill Rich Simons?' and I reply, 'Because every day for five years I said good morning to him and he never said good morning back,' and the judge says, 'I understand. You're free to go.'

"George leaving the business was devastating, and I couldn't bring myself to change the company name because, despite what he says, his contribution to the agency was enormous. However, it was as amicable a breakup as one could hope for. We respected each other and had no bad feelings. George is a great friend to this day."

Dean Mailey vividly remembers the breakup of Laurel and Hardy. "It was a big deal because Palmer Jarvis was hugely influential within the West Coast ad industry, and of course all sorts of rumours flew about how the breakup was the beginning of the end for Frank.

"But from my perspective, Frank continued to be a hunter-gatherer. His creative spark and edge remained untarnished. What really changed was the industry itself. Sharp little retail shops were rapidly giving way to corporate growth, and this, more than any breakup, affected Frank's trajectory."

I've always been interested in what gets people up in the morning, what basically turns them on. For me it's all about the importance of purpose, feeling valued or important.

In his book *Be Excellent at Anything: The Four Keys to Transforming the Way We Work and Live*, Tony Schwartz discusses two radically different meetings with leaders of two global companies. One meeting was long, dull, totally devoid of energy. The other, with a group of young Google managers, was utterly exhilarating, even after eight hours of discussion.

What accounts for the difference?

At Google, staff members felt as though they were contributing to something meaningful and larger than themselves. At the other company, the executives demonstrated no passion whatsoever for their work.

So purpose is a uniquely powerful fuel—and a source of satisfaction.

In the Broadway musical *Avenue Q*, purpose was described as the "little flame that lights a fire under your ass" (I like that expression). Purpose is grounded in contribution; it's the sense that we're headed in a clear direction for a good reason.

So, the key question should be, why are you doing what you're doing? Few of us have ever been encouraged to ask ourselves that. Why not make it the new mantra in your life—a question to which you return, over and over, as a compass for making better choices?

Yes, it's an unsettling question, but the upside is that it has the rare potential to put you on a journey to discovering the life you're truly meant to live.

—FRANK PALMER

Sixty-Nine Is a Four-Letter Word

Palmer's famous hot-dog story originated two years after he had taken decisive steps to pull Palmer Jarvis out of a creative slump, one in which observers perceived the agency to be no longer cutting edge but more of a middle-of-the-road retail shop.

Palmer had been galvanized to take action after *Strategy* magazine ranked his company the sixty-ninth best creative agency in Canada in 1992. According to Chris Staples, Palmer Jarvis staff would attend the Lotus Awards and watch while rivals such as the Vancouver office of BBDO, based in New York, stepped onstage to accept one award after another. "He and I would just sit there, having made so many submissions to the judges for consideration, and get creamed—not even nominated," he says. "This went on for three years. You know how your face burns when you're ashamed? Ours were glowing at the awards."

To make matters worse, Palmer Jarvis had created an ad to run in the latest issue of *Strategy* that depicted a jalapeño and the slogan "Almost as hot as Palmer Jarvis." Unbeknownst to staff, the ad ran alongside the company's sixty-ninth ranking. "When the issue hit the streets and we saw that, I wanted to kill myself," says Staples.

Today, Palmer still blanches at any mention of the sixty-ninth ranking, even though the low designation should by now be a distant memory. "That was downright humiliating in and of itself, but the knowledge that we were at the bottom of the Vancouver ad world, which meant nothing to the big powerhouses in Toronto and New York, was like salt rubbed in the wound," he says.

As time wore on, Palmer became obsessed with the sixty-ninth ranking, which caused him to view his career in a disturbingly different light. "There hadn't been a downward spiral that we could stop," he says. "Instead, what bothered me was the overwhelming sense that despite the decades of work and despite the partnership with George Jarvis, we'd never really gotten off the ground creatively. It was almost as if we had been deluding ourselves all these years, assuming we were way better in terms of generating cutting-edge ideas than was actually the case. The simple proof of this was that other agencies were winning awards, not us."

Losing to the competition was not only galling but, from a business perspective, also unacceptable, although one gets the impression Palmer was motivated to take action just as much to satisfy his urge to win as to protect the well-being of his company and staff.

Hilary Robertson recalls, "Frank was fed up with Palmer Jarvis having a poor creative reputation. Winning nothing year after year at the Lotus Awards show was very embarrassing for such a large agency with big clients. And we were acutely aware that Palmer Jarvis had become known around town as a 'suit' agency, meaning creativity was dictated by the account services department. The creative people pitched to the suits, and the suits then chose what they liked best and pitched to clients."

Originally from Edmonton, Staples had joined Palmer Jarvis in 1989 as an entry-level copywriter after being turned down by every other agency in Vancouver. The snubs were particularly frustrating considering that Staples had, for all intents and purposes, been born an ad man. "I'd wanted to get into the business for as long as I can remember," he says. "When I was a kid I would spend my spare time writing ads for automobiles. When it came time to go to university there were no courses in advertising, so I chose the next best thing—journalism—and in retrospect this gave me a huge advantage later in life because my first instinct was always, 'Where is the news?'"

Upon graduation Staples was hired by an agency that, he recalls, "handled a lot of government contracts and was just this side of corrupt. Later I got hired by Intergroup, which managed to steal McDonald's from Palmer Jarvis. By the time I ran into Frank at various McDonald's conventions, I had become a creative director, so when my partner and I decided to make the move to Vancouver I assumed, perhaps naively, that it would be easy to build on my career in a much bigger market. I picked the best agencies in town and began knocking on the doors."

Staples blames himself for failing to get hired by Vancouver's cream of the crop. "I had a terrible book," he says, referring to his portfolio. "I could sell work but I couldn't create it. To be honest, I was very young and to a certain degree didn't know what I was doing."

The nadir of Staples's job hunt in Vancouver came when Alvin Wasserman of Wasserman & Partners Advertising informed him that perhaps with luck he could secure employment as a junior copywriter in Calgary. When Staples finally arrived at Palmer Jarvis, his mood was black. "Even before the *Strategy* magazine ranking Palmer Jarvis was considered the worst agency in terms of creative output," he recalls. "Business was conducted over three-martini lunches, and the ads produced were cornball."

In his capacity as a creative director back in Alberta, however, Staples had occasionally rubbed shoulders with Palmer and enjoyed his enthusiasm for the business. So Staples accepted a substantial wage reduction (from the $75,000 he was earning annually in Alberta to $55,000 as a lowly copywriter) and joined the team. He recalls, "Years later, I learned that a Palmer Jarvis partner in Edmonton phoned Frank prior to my being hired and warned him, 'You know Chris Staples is gay, don't you?' This was back in the day when gays were viewed through a radically different lens than is the case now. But Frank replied, 'Yeah, so what? I like the guy, plus he's talented.'

"Needless to say, I liked Frank enormously, and as I got to know him better I realized that despite his jocularity he truly didn't have any prejudices. As long as you had talent and worked hard, all he cared about was if you liked him."

Still, Staples hadn't arrived at the ideal time to become acquainted with his new boss. "I'd heard all the stories about his pranks and gags, but not once during my tenure did he pull any, at least not to my knowledge," he says. "I think he was a bit fed up with his jokester reputation, and certainly he had the company's dismal reputation to worry about. Frank had worked hard all his life, now he wanted the respect that was due to him."

Finally, in 1992, Palmer decided to enlist industry veteran Ron Woodall, who had also been the creative director of Expo 86, to help revamp his firm. "One of Woodall's many accomplishments in the ad world was the creation of the A&W bear mascot," says Palmer. "I recruited him because I needed a creative director who would act as a sort of teacher, guiding staff and training a lot of new talent."

As is the case with so many advertising greats, Ron Woodall hasn't been given his proper due by the digital media. Raised in Montreal, Woodall became an accomplished painter and a well-known photographer. He rose to prominence by working for McKim in that city (the advertising agency that, among many other achievements, created the Chevron slogan "Your town pump"), and he moved west in the 1960s to handle the Scott Paper account for J. Walter Thompson Canada.

Woodall, who in his later years assumed the appearance of a white-haired, white-bearded bear, had well earned the reputation of being a hellraiser. One especially memorable misadventure involved Cominco, an account belonging to McKim's industrial division. The division's manager, Jimmy Sheppard, had arranged a display of Cominco's sacrificial zinc anodes in the McKim boardroom, along with glass bowls of fresh and salt water filled with galvanized and ungalvanized screws, to demonstrate how Cominco zincs prevented corrosion.

Sheppard was going to photograph the display for print publication, but the night prior Woodall and a colleague, Graham

Watt, staggered into the boardroom after an evening of heavy drinking. Intent on mischief, Woodall removed the ungalvanized screws and sprayed them with enough fixative to ward off any corrosion. He then poured out the bowls containing salt water and refilled them with 7-up. Finally, he urinated in the bowl with the galvanized screws before staggering out of the boardroom and headed homeward.

The following morning Sheppard and the president of Cominco entered the boardroom; upon noticing that the place cards indicating which were the salt-water bowls seemed mismatched, the president dipped his finger into the bowl in which Woodall had urinated and licked it: "This one for sure, Jim!"

Palmer admits that Woodall's role wasn't universally accepted within the corridors of the agency. "There were a lot of people who said, 'What does this old fart know?' But they soon found out they were learning from the best. Woodall didn't mince words or edit his thoughts, which is exactly what we needed. Sometimes it was tough even for me to hear what he had to say."

Woodall, who now lives on Bowen Island, remembers Palmer Jarvis as "typically service-oriented and suffering a serious product quality problem and a bad creative reputation. It had been that way for a long time. Still, despite lacking creative strength, it was a successful and profitable business.

Woodall initially didn't know what to expect of Palmer but soon realized that he would be remarkably cooperative. "He wished to jump-start the creative product and eventually make it the best on Canada's West Coast. This mandate meant going literally from worst to best. Full management support was promised."

Initially, Woodall wanted to close the agency while he determined how best to fix it, but Palmer insisted that business continue as usual, meaning Woodall would be a constant, lurking presence in the Palmer Jarvis hallways and offices.

Woodall says that because the mandate was so ambitious, it was difficult deciding where to begin. "If doable at all, this last-to-first objective seemed a ten-year process at best, even if management stayed the course no matter what the pressure was to revert. Certainly, the creative department was not a happy place. There was cynicism and internal conflict and little sense of team. This department had too long worked totally under the account group's thumb."

As with all corporate renaissance projects, the first order of business was to formulate a vision statement. "Over the years, Frank Palmer had tried to document his thoughts on the kind of agency he would like," says Woodall. "There was a fair archive of 'The Thoughts of Frank.' While they were rambling, Frank's writings fell into three distinct piles. In the first pile was his desire for his agency to be seen as different from the others and doing things differently. The second pile bemoaned the ad industry's lack of respect for Palmer Jarvis and how Frank wanted the agency to be looked up to as a role model. The third pile was mostly about leadership.

"It was questionable whether any vision slogan would remedy the status quo, but we fashioned 'Be Unique, Be Respected, Be a Leader.'"

Chris Staples recalls Woodall's modus operandi fondly. "Ron was six years older than Frank, and established quite a physical presence in our headquarters. He would sit in his office, which was very dark and contained an early computer, listen to everyone and tell the most amazing stories about his career experiences. He became my champion, and the stories he told me about his past gave me the confidence I so badly needed at that time, since I still felt that to a large degree I was faking it.

"All Ron did for six solid months was take notes. That was it: He produced volumes. I think he viewed the entire Palmer Jarvis operation as a fascinating social dynamic."

Woodall tackled Palmer Jarvis's rejuvenation with two ideas in mind: awards are the most important thing in the advertising business, and creative people are free agents motivated solely by the success of their own careers. "Most of the success to come would actually flow from these two truths, though to this day the validity of the strategy still seems absurd and heretical," he says.

He adds that the notion of awards being the most important thing in advertising was initially proposed with tongue planted firmly in cheek. "But any observation of industry behaviour bears it out. A gain in a client's market share is not likely to send the agency crowd off to France in tuxedos and ball gowns. Instead, the social schedule of advertising is built around awards. Agencies run full-page trade ads on the occasion of a Gold Lion or two, and every year our industry celebrates about two dozen of these little Olympics. The quickest and perhaps the only way to quickly shift an agency's reputation is the awards game."

Woodall elaborates on the psychology behind winning awards. "Most creative types had little genuine interest in the selling effectiveness of the work. At least, if they did, they didn't much talk about it. On the other hand, the winning of awards was clearly an obsession. And why not? That is how creatives prosper, how superstars are identified. Here's my test: either you can write a campaign that will raise our biggest client's brand share by five points, or you can have a Gold Lion at Cannes. The fact is that creatives are hired by other creatives who stay very aware of such things as award counts. By definition, creative careers are fuelled by the level of celebrity achieved."

It's a credit to Woodall's expertise and sheer gut-level know-how that early on he had a clear battle plan of how Palmer Jarvis could start winning awards, and the plan hinged on the core belief that the agency needed to become its own most important client. "It would actually have to put its own welfare ahead of that of its clients, in the sense that client budgets would be the fuel to fire our award aspirations," he says. "The mindset adopted within the creative department was awards at any cost."

Woodall notes that although it was strictly an internal subject that account management did not want to hear or talk about, the open focus on award winning produced a fascinating effect on creative performance and product. "Every day, hundreds of agencies write mission statements promising creative priority, but they are seldom able to get beyond the rhetoric because of business as usual. The trick in our case was to actually do it in a way that would be recognized and counted as identifiable scoring in the 'who's most creative' game.

"We came to regard the agency very much as the client, the awards jury became the consumer and each creative person's own career became the end product. The writers and art directors were encouraged to regard the building of a great 'book' as their key objective. Each one knew that he would be judged primarily on awards performance, and we fired and recruited on that basis alone. Every assignment was looked upon as an opportunity, not so much to sell product, but to build a career."

During his overhaul of the office culture, Woodall suggested that Staples become the agency's creative director, based on his leadership skills and his ability to energize other creative people with his enthusiasm. "To say I was surprised was an understate-ment, because I was thirty-three and still felt new to the business," says Staples. "However, Ron had been giving me words of encour-agement during his months of note taking, so I imagine he had been grooming me for the role to some degree. And I found myself eager to take it on."

Woodall and Staples installed new processes aimed at promo-ting superior work, the most significant of which was a peer review system that subjected each creative team's efforts to critiques from other members of the department, as well as from people in the media. And because one aspect of the cultural shift meant bring-ing in people who wanted to fight for good ads instead of merely pleasing the client, a highly talented and fearless man named Tom Shepansky, who had gained experience at two Edmonton ad agencies (and who would co-found his own agency, Rethink, in 1999), was recruited as an account director.

Although preferring to give Woodall and colleagues wide latitude, Palmer pitched in when he was needed. Staples later con-fessed to *BCBusiness* magazine that he was "scared shitless because I'd never created an award-winning ad," so Palmer accelerated Staples's learning by sending him to industry conferences and pairing him with art directors Mark Mizgala (a new recruit from Miller Myers Bruce Dalla Costa in Toronto) and Ian Grais (who later would co-found Rethink with Shepansky). "Underscoring all of this activity was a tremendous mutual sense of confidence that Frank would never quash the emerging sense of freedom everyone was feeling," Staples recalls. "He was 100 per cent supportive and never once freaked out, no matter what Ron proposed."

Hilary Robertson says, "Ron made changes to the personnel in the creative department—hires and fires. The company was changing and the atmosphere became exciting. People were really charged up about the possibilities. Part of the process was making everyone feel some responsibility for the end creative product. However, for some people these changes were difficult and there was a lot of staff turnover. Hires were made carefully and the deadwood was cut away."

For Robertson, it was like being part of an entirely new organization. "I loved working at the agency during this time; it was a lot of fun, very challenging and motivating."

Woodall agrees: "A lot of people came and went. The pace had quickened and the expectations rose. There was a natural attrition of people who were uncomfortable with the change or just didn't get what was happening. The growing influence of the creative department also encouraged and demanded a shift to the recruitment of a new breed of younger, faster, hipper account people who showed sensitivity and guts, and were passionate about the work.

"Advertising was obviously not something that happened only in the creative department; suit input was no longer regarded as tampering. We hoped that more people, including clients, would join in the evolution. And it happened. There was genuine excitement over actually being a part of what one signed off on."

An example of the new creativity was the tremendously popular "Humongous Bank" campaign created for Richmond Savings, which ran from 1995 to 1999. The campaign's fictitious bank illustrated the difference between the small and friendly Richmond credit union and the big banking institutions, with slogans such as "Your money is our money" and "We built this bank one service charge at a time."

Although the Canadian Bankers Association complained that the ads insulted banking employees, the public didn't agree, and the client base of Richmond Savings doubled during the campaign's four-year run.

Woodall elaborates on the recruitment of new blood at Palmer Jarvis. "Our prime avoidance was big ego. The ideal hire was a young up-and-comer who would kill to improve his book but was being underused or mistreated by his current agency. We also raided the grad classes of the best ad schools for interns. The idea was to get them fresh and train them our way. Like puppies.

"More important than getting good puppies was keeping them long enough to imprint Palmer Jarvis as their permanent home. So we tried to provide the ideal working environment. We made the organizational structure quite horizontal in that we downplayed hierarchy and layering. All opinions were respected as equally valid. There was no fear of going too far or being too radical. No idea was a bad one. There was a lot of mentoring."

One result of this strategy was that, according to Woodall, "For the first five glorious years, we did not lose one creative that we wanted to keep. The original dream, in fact—to craft a creative Mecca in Vancouver that could attract and keep remarkably talented people from around the world—almost seemed to be happening."

Woodall describes yet another vital factor in Palmer Jarvis's spectacular turnabout: "Right or wrong, we were averse to research. Because so much research seemed to skew against the new idea, we feared that pretesting might scuttle much of the kind of work we were doing. Focus groups, we believed, are people who believe nothing should be done for the first time, so the only focus group we respected was an awards jury. When there was information to help us understand the consumer we welcomed it, but we resisted research that threatened to shape the concept or make it harder to win awards."

On a daily basis, the feedback Palmer Jarvis staff paid the most attention to was the internal critique. "We relied heavily on peer review, which the industry press credited us with inventing," says Woodall. "It was actually our attempt to eliminate what I call 'boss-ism.' While our system seemed to fascinate the industry, it is a simple, common-sense practice. The department became an open shooting gallery in which all work in progress was at any time fair game for critique. At regular weekly sessions, creative groups presented current projects for no-holds-barred review. Criticism was tough but constructive and impersonal. These were 'drop your pants' sessions in which you dared not show the mediocre."

For his part, Palmer stood in the middle of all this cataclysmic change and forced himself to think positively. "I was optimistic about our future only because we were the sixty-ninth most creative agency in Canada, so there was no choice but to improve."

Despite the culture shift and ambitious front-loading of talent, the revitalization of Palmer Jarvis wouldn't have worked if the agency hadn't acquired new clients who supported the unconventional advertising ideas that were soon flowing from Palmer's reinvigorated staff. Acquiring the right clients was partly luck and partly hard work, and frequently staff didn't know how accommodating these clients would actually be until after a pitch had been delivered. Palmer complained to *Strategy* magazine during the revamp: "Too many clients out there don't have the guts to go with agency recommendations. Too much research is being done, and too often great ideas are getting sifted out."

But Staples points out that a lot of old clients like SunRype (which had become a Palmer Jarvis account after the merger with Rich Simons) and Richmond Savings remained with the company, and that they were equally enthusiastic about the re-vamped Palmer Jarvis's edgy approach to advertising. "The reason for this was simple: just as we had recruited new blood, our clients were doing the same for their organizations. For example, Hugh Ruthven was a Young Turk at McDonald's who was eager to shake things up. The same goes for Brent Cuthbertson, the new creative director at Richmond Savings. It really was a case of perfect timing that enabled our re-energized agency to move forward."

As a British Columbia Institute of Technology student, Hugh Ruthven had worked for Palmer Jarvis on a practicum in 1981. He became a field account executive working the McDonald's accounts, and he moved over to the fast-food giant in 1986. "I stayed there until '94, having graduated from ad manager to dir-ector of marketing," he says. "Chris is correct in stating that we were extremely receptive to different ways of getting our message across." At Palmer's invitation, Ruthven rejoined the agency as a partner in 1994.

Woodall recalls that at critical times, management was ag-gressively supporting "edgy work" that in the past they would never have considered. "We discussed having a client list tailored to our product rather than vice versa. This was tough talk in a small market. And we were no longer reminded that we were not in the business of winning awards, which to the creative people had always seemed very funny to say anyhow."

Physical working conditions changed too. "In 1995, the clut-tered old Palmer Jarvis offices were vacated for what seemed to us an absolutely knockout new workspace," says Woodall. "Tiny jail-cell offices were replaced by light and openness. There was a feel-good sense of space and freedom. From almost anywhere, there were unobstructed views of Vancouver's sea and mountains. The custom-designed rooms to house the creative teams had big funky sliding barn doors."

The switch to a new workspace was important on many levels. "The move served as a clear notice of change," says Woodall. "It speeded the demise of the old culture. It repackaged the agency. Creative had big input into the new space. We got to design our own environment. One of the first moves was to flip creative from being downstairs from the executive row to being upstairs. The symbolism was pretty clear."

Woodall stresses that contrary to appearances, there was control in the creative department. "We approached assignments like everyone else does. Strategic planning was taken very seriously. The consumer was respected, despite our internal rhetoric. Still, in peer reviews the first question remained, Will it win an award? It was not enough to merely meet strategy and get client approval. The more difficult hurdle was that it must be achieved with remarkable ingenuity of craft. We tried to be tougher judges of pure creative performance than our clients would ever be. It was not enough to aspire to communicate effectively; it was also critical to do so with remarkable craftsmanship."

The revamped Palmer Jarvis was also a fun place to be. Woodall recalls, "In the early years, there seemed to be a constant cacophony of positive mayhem. There was an astonishing level of good vibes. The dress code was very Honolulu flip-flop. Meetings got hysterical. We partied often. There were island retreats with lots of beer and tequila. These people stayed close friends after work. Some became couples."

Arguably, the ad campaign that received the most attention during the post-revitalization years (and that Staples and his colleagues masterminded) was for Greyhound Air, a division of the Greyhound bus line that was established to compete with BC's fledgling WestJet service. "We made our pitch in Calgary to the head of the company, who was a stern, no-nonsense Dutchman, and to his colleagues, who were equally dour," Palmer says. "The pitch consisted of me describing a television commercial that would show a close-up of an airplane wheel. Along comes a greyhound, who lifts his leg and pees against it, followed by the tag, 'Greyhound Air: marking new territory.'"

The punchline was met with stony silence. "I stood there slowly dying," Palmer recalls. "There wasn't so much as a smile from anyone, just these cold eyes fixed on me. This lasted for maybe ten seconds, although it seemed more like ten minutes. Then finally one board member clears his throat and says, 'I think that's fucking fantastic.' Everyone agreed, including the president, and we went on to create one of our most successful and controversial campaigns."

What was at the core of the revitalized Palmer Jarvis ads? "We chose to take a retro approach, digging back to the '60s," explains Woodall. "The idea was to introduce—or steal—the style of my heroes, Bill Bernbach, George Lois and Helmut Krone, from the glory days of Doyle Dane Bernbach, now known as DDB. That would be our philosophy and look, but in fresh hands and minds. Like them, we went for simplicity. We used minimal elements and as few words as possible to convey a concept. We eliminated extraneous embellishment and trickiness. We made edgy humour based on irony and hyperbole our calling card. Mostly, we stayed sparse and droll. Today, everyone tries sparse and droll.

"We decided there would never be tight comps or storyboards. We would not test concepts to death and we did not make ripomatics [an assemblage of video footage keyed to music intended to give viewers an idea of the finished product]. A concept had to be explainable in one sentence. We used the roughest of pencil roughs when selling to clients. We felt that the idea was everything and if we couldn't convey it with a couple of pencil lines, then it wasn't worth embellishing with a fortune of storyboarding. Art directors did not touch the Macs until there was a concept that had survived the internal review. We forced concept over technique in every way possible."

Woodall was hardly shy about upsetting people. "We also tried, as much as possible, to present only the recommended concept and not offer multiple choices or bouquets of ideas. If a great concept was rejected, we tried to eliminate the opportunity to choose the weaker alternative. We would discuss the reasons and then return with another great campaign but not have back-pocket seconds. This, of course, was a great hackle raiser.

"We actually believed there were no bad assignments. Even the most difficult throwaway projects were considered potential award winners, extra bullets, so we always treated them that way. Our juniors, who tended to inherit such jobs, were brilliant and consistently proved us right. We didn't expect a home run every time, but we expected a swing for a home run every time."

Woodall adds that everyone tried to stay fluid. "Creative teams and their accounts were switched regularly. No one got stale on an account. No one got stale with a partner. The creative department thrived on openness and shared information. Everyone knew what was going on."

In this reinvigorated atmosphere, Palmer's talent for investigation became especially acute, to the point where he knew what would happen in the corporate world long before the word got out on the street. This too benefited Palmer Jarvis, as proven by the time Palmer found out that his client Safeway would be relocating its marketing operation from Winnipeg to San Francisco—something the marketing director in Winnipeg didn't even know about yet. Armed with this early knowledge, Palmer quickly pitched to then rival Save-On-Foods and won the account.

Throughout Palmer Jarvis's retooling, management stayed remarkably supportive of the creative group's awards focus. "They backed us in taking on whichever client would allow great work," says Woodall. "These were often small under-the-radar accounts with no possibility of generating revenue, but this was sometimes the price of fast-tracking to some measure of fame and respectability. The bottom line was sometimes traded for the new notoriety, and monumental award show budgets had to be approved."

Despite maintaining an analytical stance and deploying his strategies methodically, Woodall got swept up in the overall excitement of rebuilding Palmer Jarvis. "The agency's clients began to get much better product for exactly the same price," he says. "Often they got famous advertising that everyone talked about and made the evening newscast. This had rarely happened in the past. Palmer Jarvis was finally producing some great work. It was becoming a noted creative agency, building a respectable reputation in Vancouver and beyond."

Strategy magazine's annual ranking of Canadian agencies on a point system (which is tied to national and international award show performance) says it all:

- In 1992 Palmer Jarvis was ranked the 69th creative agency in Canada with 3 points.
- In 1993 it was ranked 27th with 16 points.

- In 1994 it was ranked 9th with 44 points.
- In 1995 it was ranked 6th with 104 points.
- In 1996 it was ranked 3rd with 192 points.
- In 1997 it was ranked 1st with 346 points.
- In 1998 it was ranked 1st with 450 points.
- In 1999 it was ranked 1st with 490 points.
- In 2000 it was ranked 1st with 506 points.
- In 2001 it was ranked 1st with 516 points.
- In 2002 it was ranked 1st with 427 points.
- In 2003 it was ranked 1st with 618 points.
- In 2004 it was ranked 1st with 587 points.

To put this long series of numbers into context, by the time Palmer Jarvis scored 506 points in 2000, the second-ranked agency, BBDO, scored only 168.

A triumph of a different sort occurred in 1995, when the national trade magazine *Marketing* named Palmer Jarvis as Canada's Agency of the Year. It was a first-ever designation for a West Coast shop.

* * *

Marika Bujdoso fell into Palmer's orbit in 1992, when Palmer was debating how to combat award snubs and low magazine rankings. Raised on Vancouver Island, Marika had moved to Vancouver as a nutritionist and fitness instructor, and her first glimpse of Palmer was at Gold's Gym in North Vancouver.

Typically, he exhibited none of the stress that was plaguing him at work. "I was an administrator and he walked into the office to talk to a colleague, but I also think he was checking me out," she recalls. "He was handsome and had good colour, but what struck me the most was the sense of power he exuded. It's something all truly successful men have, and he had it in abundance.

"A few months later a female friend asked if I was going to his barbecue party. When I confessed I hadn't been invited she said, 'Please come with me. I don't want to go alone because Frank's interested in me—but he's really not my type, plus he's way too old!'"

Later, after Marika obtained a licence as a real estate agent and was working as an operations manager for Drake International Business Centre, she met Palmer more formally when her friend, Allan Black, an account representative for Palmer Jarvis, invited her to a dinner party that included Bob Stamnes and Hugh Ruthven, as well as her future husband. "Frank and I shared great conversation, but I was blushing and had butterflies," she says. "In short, I was totally hooked on him. A few weeks later I went to a party at his house in the British Properties. The guests left one by one as the night wore on; I stayed, and the rest is history."

Marika was quickly initiated into Palmer's roller-coaster lifestyle, starting with a fancy cocktail party she attended (and which Palmer decided to crash with six other people, wearing full camouflage combat gear plus green and black face makeup) and culminating when he met Marika's parents. "My mom, who was also named Marika, was three years younger than Frank and absolutely gorgeous, with long black hair and dressed that day in a miniskirt," she says. "He stared at her when they shook hands, kept staring at her after we all sat down, and finally she asked me to join her in the bathroom. 'If he doesn't stop staring at me, I swear I'll say something rude,' she said, and I replied, 'Mom, I think he's admiring your beauty and he probably wants to paint you.'"

Marika laughs at the memory. "It was an awkward situation because although I'd told my parents Frank was older than me, I didn't tell them he was in fact nineteen years older. But they loved him at first sight nonetheless, despite him gaping at Mom in a miniskirt."

Marika even had the capacity to overlook some of Palmer's quirkier peccadilloes. "If we were together, he would walk through a door first instead of holding it open for me, which was something he did no matter who he was with. And if he was sitting down and a woman walked in, he would greet her without getting up. Initially that shocked me, but I soon realized he wasn't being rude. He was just being Frank. Perhaps it had to do with his being an only child, but none of these quirks were malicious."

In the months leading up to their wedding, Marika exerted her influence over him, predominantly in the area of physical fitness. "He was strong to begin with and big on weight training, but I did things like make him decrease his weightlifting and increase his cardiovascular routines, as well as get him to develop healthier eating habits," she says, adding that her strong-willed Hungarian heritage combined with a healthy temper compelled Palmer to do as told.

Ironically, Marika's obsession with improving her husband's health would, years later, contribute to one of the few genuine sore spots of her marriage: Palmer's seemingly inexhaustible capacity for work. "I'm well aware that the healthier he is, the more time he spends at the office or on the road and the less time with me," she says.

Marika also set about steering Palmer away from people she felt were taking advantage of him professionally and personally. Although the stories of Marika confronting such people are almost as numerous as the stories of Palmer's gags (mainly because the confrontations tended to unfold in highly public places), all Marika will say about the subject is, "I got rid of them. Plenty of people formed an opinion of me as a result, but I didn't care; Frank was my knight in shining armour, and I wanted to protect him."

Palmer benefited from Marika's company in other ways. "I understood his passion for buying and selling real estate since I was in the business too," she explains. "He's a genius with numbers, so he didn't learn anything from me in this regard. However, I have a really good sense of when to buy and sell, so we made a good team."

＊　　＊　　＊

In 1993, in the midst of Palmer's new life as a married man and just as the Palmer Jarvis resurrection was gaining traction, long-time client Woodward's went bankrupt. "We were doing all their ads, flyers, newspaper and television advertising, and when they went under they owed me $750,000, which I needed to pay off the outstanding accounts we had with the media," Palmer says.

That kind of tab, if not taken care of immediately, would be large enough to sink the agency for good. Palmer went into crisis mode and quickly concocted a plan: staff would receive pay cuts of 5, 10 and 15 per cent, depending on their salaries, and some staff members would be laid off.

Palmer then phoned *The Vancouver Sun*, CKNW and the other media outlets he owed money to and asked to pay them back over the next three years. Any advertising he booked in the meantime would be paid under normal circumstances.

The only thing that would enable this bold plan to be endorsed was Palmer's reputation as a businessman. Fortunately, the local media held him in high regard. They signed off on the deal, and he wound up paying them back in two years instead of three. "All I cared about was getting myself out of a dangerous predicament, but my strategy earned Palmer Jarvis the best credit rating in the city," he says. "I even got an award for paying back the money."

"Palmer standing up and taking it on the chin and paying back all these people out of his own pocket made me respect him enormously," Bob Bryant recalls. "You could say all you wanted about his aggressiveness and outrageous antics, and I certainly did at the time. But he showed his true colours during that incident."

The Woodward's disaster also made Marika understand her role as Palmer's wife. "It was a crisis that demanded his full attention," she says. "It struck me that if I kept track of his social commitments and managed the homestead, he would have the freedom to focus his energy wherever it was most needed."

Marika admits that she sometimes felt she was being too strict with her husband. "But honestly, knowing his previous experience with other people, I felt I had to keep cracking the whip to keep him committed."

Meanwhile, Palmer Jarvis was earning the respect of rival agencies for its ad campaigns. "Chris Staples deserves a lot of credit for making these campaigns unorthodox and cutting edge," says Palmer. "Creatively he was and still is one of the very best ad men in the business."

One of Staples's early efforts was a coupon ad for Ginsana, a ginseng-based energy drink. As would be the case with subsequent campaigns, Staples' creativity was in full blossom: the ad consisted simply of a big dotted square containing a headline: "Too Tired to Rip Out This Coupon?"

Ian Grais told *Strategy* magazine that most of Palmer Jarvis's inspirations were born of necessity: "In Los Angeles, you can have a mediocre idea and attach amazing talent to that idea, and that idea will get better. We don't have huge budgets, so we work hard to make sure our ideas are strong out of the gate."

Being edgy and cheeky had an enduring payoff: along with other local agencies such as TBWA and BBDO that were creating similar ads, Palmer Jarvis ushered in what became known in other parts of Canada as the "Vancouver School" of advertising. "Another term for it was 'Bratvertising,' which I loved," says Staples. "It drove the Toronto people mad—with envy, no doubt."

Palmer's humiliation over being named the sixty-ninth best creative agency in Canada had resulted in him being largely responsible for making Vancouver a force to be reckoned with on the national advertising scene. And it wouldn't have happened had he not been willing to acknowledge his limitations, step aside and let Ron Woodall work his magic.

The success dovetailed nicely with Vancouver's rapid maturation as an urban centre. In the late 1990s more and more suburbanites were moving back into the city and stimulating business, Pacific Rim trade was at an all-time high, and the film production and high-tech sectors were flourishing. Vancouver was still small as an international destination, but it was high on the list of places that people wanted to do business with. In this regard Palmer helped propel the city into the twenty-first century. He was the quintessential local boy who had made good.

Alan Gee discusses the significance of Palmer's achievement. "I immigrated to Toronto from England in the 1970s, and for a long time our perception of Vancouver was that of a backwater—that is, if we had any perception of it at all," he says. "I knew Vancouver vaguely as the place where Howard Hughes holed up when he was going nuts. Nothing much happened there and probably never would, because all the talent was here in Toronto and we were the epicentre of the Canadian advertising world. That was our mindset. It wasn't a snobbery stemming from a dislike of the West Coast; instead we simply thought there was nothing much out there beyond great scenery and clement weather.

"But then Palmer Jarvis appeared on the radar as kind of a western outpost. And then the 1990s came and the revitalized Palmer Jarvis made everyone sit up and take notice. Subsequently, when Frank transitioned his firm into DDB, he became the number-one ad man in Canada, and everyone else was a distant second."

Gee marvels at what this took. "Some would say energy, but I would say ferocity—Frank's maniacal insistence on winning and getting ahead at any cost. I'm aware of the problems George Jarvis had dealing with Frank on a daily basis, and I know a lot of competitors got their noses out of joint over the stunts he pulled. But any truly successful business person has a degree of ruthlessness that is absolutely essential in enabling him or her to stand apart from the pack."

Gee points out that Palmer's achievement is even more noteworthy considering that Palmer was no longer a young man. "He did all this at a time when many successful people become complacent," Gee says. "Plus, the older you get in this business, the less the younger talent think you're capable of being innovative. I know that personally, because with my agency I'm constantly telling my younger guys who think I can't develop a cutting-edge slogan to fuck off.

"But it's not as if Frank defies age; instead, he simply doesn't realize the years are going by, and because he doesn't realize this, time has no effect on him. He has all the energy and anger of his youth, so to a large degree the younger folk listen to what he has to say."

*   *   *

One of Palmer's biggest campaigns in terms of sheer size, complexity and cost occurred as a result of the Hudson's Bay Company's celebration of its 325th anniversary in 1995. In an attempt to seek inspiration for what needed to be an unforgettable media event, Palmer convinced Barry Agnew, the Bay's then-senior vice president of marketing, his colleagues and other promotions people to join him on a cross-country train trip. "We figured we would get fabulous ideas by following the route of the explorers," Palmer recalls. "But soon after the train left the station, I realized that no matter how hard you stared through the windows there was really fuck-all to see except the back end of houses and barns. Plus, except for the Rockies, Canada is pretty flat."

Palmer also had to endure plumes of smoke emanating from his companions, who lit up with alarming frequency. "By the time we approached Ontario there wasn't anything in my luggage I could wear that didn't reek of cigarettes."

Palmer's wardrobe may have been spoiled, and instead of being uplifted by majestic scenery he felt like a sardine in a tin. But when his party disembarked in Toronto, he had come up with a killer idea: to stage an outdoor concert featuring the biggest names in Canadian music.

He promptly flew back home and started making calls. "It took a hell of a lot of planning, but in the end we rented a farmer's field in High River, Alberta, and to that field came Bryan Adams, Gordon Lightfoot, Burton Cummings, Anne Murray—twenty performers in all. It was a once-in-a-lifetime event for Canadian music lovers."

Palmer underplays the complexity of putting together such a show, from dealing with the different talent managers representing the stars to finding sponsors (it was later disclosed that the Prime Minister's Office of Jean Chrétien overrode bureaucratic objections to award a $500,000 sponsorship to the concert.

However, the three-day Big Sky concert was a smash, drawing seventy-five thousand attendees and raising about $1 million for HBC's Adventurers' Foundation for Youth, and Palmer followed up with television commercials commemorating the company's anniversary.

Palmer will discuss only in confidence the amount of money it took to stage Big Sky and shoot the commercials. Bryan Adams's salary alone was a small fortune, and when asked if he thinks HBC earned a good return on its investment, Palmer replies, "If you're talking about determining a dollar-for-dollar return and figuring out a profit margin, that's almost impossible to do. Certainly HBC got enormous exposure, but to what extent that directly caused an increase in retail foot traffic is unclear."

Aware that some critics are appalled by the huge sums of money big agencies spend in the name of promotion, Palmer offers the following: "All I can say about Big Sky is that it highlights the unavoidable truth that advertising is a risk. The American merchant John Wanamaker, who is considered to be one of the pioneers of marketing, once said, 'Half the money I spend on advertising is wasted; the trouble is, I don't know which half.' We use all sorts of measurements and calculations to determine the success of any campaign, but at the end of the day it's still a risk. Our entire industry hinges on the trust between the ad men and their clients, and thankfully Barry Agnew was so trusting of us he wouldn't even show up to watch the filming of his commercials."

The sacrifices required by Palmer Jarvis to gain trust from a client were sometimes substantial. Case in point: upon pitching a series of commercials to Mohawk Canada Ltd. president William Duncan and other upper-management types, Palmer sensed that despite the overall enthusiasm in the room, Duncan was ill at ease.

Palmer returned to his office with the ad campaign fully approved, but a voice in the back of his head compelled him to phone Duncan and ask what was making him uncomfortable. Duncan searched for an answer but couldn't pinpoint the source of his discomfort. "I basically trust my peoples' judgment, and I trust yours," he replied uneasily.

Palmer thought about how much money had been poured into the development of the commercials by his team. It was not an unsubstantial amount, and he knew they were good. Moreover, Duncan was willing to proceed with their production. But the tone of Duncan's voice told him that going ahead would be a mistake. "Bill," he said with false bravado, "I'm not going to let you accept the commercials. Go to your marketing director and tell him to phone my team and say we need to develop new ones."

The marketing director did so, and Palmer played dumb when a colleague informed him of the news. "I replied, 'Jesus, we'd better crank out new commercials then,'" he recalls. "So we did, and after it was all over I could have sold Bill Duncan pink flamingos if I'd wanted to."

*   *   *

In 1997, five years after being listed by *Strategy* magazine as the sixty-ninth best creative agency, Palmer Jarvis was ranked first in the country by the same magazine. That same year at the Lotus Awards the company was named Agency of the Year and collected so many trophies that its banquet table collapsed.

Other accolades poured in. "At one point, Palmer Jarvis had a streak of eleven consecutive new business wins," says Ron Woodall. "In 1996 and 1997 we took silver for *Strategy*'s Creative Agency of the Year. In 1997 we were *Marketing* magazine's Agency of the Year for the second time in three years. By then, we had dominated the Lotus Awards for the fourth year in a row. More importantly, and for the first time in 1997, we dominated the National Marketing Awards in Toronto, Canada's defining creative show, winning 80 per cent of the gold awards. We also led Canada in wins at Cannes and many other venues."

After the revitalization of Palmer Jarvis, Palmer felt open enough to share how his agency approached work day by day. "We're in touch with what's taking place all the time," he told *Strategy* magazine in his best classic ad-man manner. "We do store checks. We go into the marketplace. Talk to people. We do a lot of research. If you don't get out of your office, you don't know what the hell's going on . . .

"We also have a checking measure in place whereby we ask the client to review us. We give them a form asking them how we're doing. If there are flaws in some of the areas of doing business, the client has the chance to say so."

Many industry observers assumed that Palmer had reached the summit of his ambitions—indeed, the pinnacle of what he was physically capable of doing. But during the years it took to resurrect his agency, Palmer was also plotting its ultimate future. Several months after the sweep at the Lotus Awards he surprised the ad world once more by undertaking what he famously calls "the best thing I ever did and also the worst thing I ever did."

Think of your reputation as your most important asset. Reputation is the most fundamental and important asset of companies, officials and employees. If you've been reading the newspaper or watching TV lately, you've heard all about wasteful government spending, non-compliance or even fraud. Once someone has been tarnished with allegations of misconduct, the reputation might stick no matter how hard he or she tries to correct it.

Warren Buffett said, "It takes twenty years to build a reputation and five minutes to ruin it. If you think about that, you'll do things differently."

I believe that having a great reputation is your most important asset, and it can be gained by following through on all the things you promise to do. Having this type of reputation helps make you trustworthy even before you meet people or prospective clients.

In some circles it's called being "social proof."

Trust me, it makes good sense.

— FRANK PALMER

Going Global

Any achiever has his or her share of hangers-on and yes-men, and Palmer is no exception, although they tend to be part of Vancouver's larger social scene rather than the rank and file within his own company.

In terms of his career, however, Palmer is almost universally revered, and this comes at a price: few if any people feel completely at ease criticizing him. Few, that is, except for Hilary Robertson.

Robertson's career with Palmer spanned the early post–George Jarvis years, extended through the Palmer Jarvis revitalization and continued into the DDB era before ending in 2010, just two years before Palmer Jarvis DDB was renamed DDB Canada. "I became Frank's executive assistant after Rich Simons left the agency, and the chats Frank used to have with me when he visited Rich made us both realize we were comfortable enough with each other to forge a good working relationship," she says. "It turned out to be a great relationship, to the point where Frank eventually gave me a lot of authority to act on his behalf. "

Robertson started her career at a time when letters had to be typed from handwritten notes. "My job consisted of producing and editing a lot of documents, setting up meetings, organizing events and helping to facilitate the workload of the administrative staff, which back then was just under twenty in number," she says.

Of all the people in his inner circle, Palmer half-jokingly refers to Robertson "as the one person who could easily do me in," and Robertson half-jokingly agrees. "Over the years I was exposed to everything: the love affairs, the fights, the deals, the plots, you name it," she says. "I've lost track of how many instances I've heard every one of Frank's stories. And I got to know him better than most people because of the sheer amount of time we spent together."

Still, even though Robertson has formed theories as to why Palmer acts the way he does, to this day she can't shake the sense that she hasn't uncovered the whole truth about him. "I think the real Frank is a well-guarded secret," she says. "He'll tell what he chooses people to know about him, just as he'll teach younger talent what they need to know but not everything he has learned."

Being adaptable and accepting, Robertson found it easy to deal with Palmer's personal peccadilloes. "But I can also be dreadful, direct and harsh, so he always knew what was on my mind," she says. "For example, I didn't think all of his jokes were funny. In fact, he pulled a stunt at my expense when my mother was dying of cancer that got me so upset I walked out and didn't come back for a few days. When I next saw him, I said if he did that again I'd leave for good. He was extremely contrite and sent flowers to my home that evening."

When asked if she thought Palmer's contriteness was genuine, Robertson replies, "Of course. Well, yes." After a pause, she adds, "Put it this way: as genuinely contrite as he could be. He needed me, so he had to be contrite. And I forgave his faults because he was a likeable, talented, impossible, complex person who stuck up for his team without fail."

Hugh Ruthven, who is an open admirer of Palmer, concedes that sometimes Palmer's misjudgments could be monumental. "But he always had best intentions at heart," he says. "I'll never forget when he invited the hockey player Tiger Williams to the headquarters to give everyone a pep talk. He didn't bother reviewing what Williams was going to say beforehand, so the very first thing Williams did in front of an audience of over a hundred people was tell a derogatory joke about gays." Laughing, Ruthven adds, "You could have heard a pin drop. Frank's face was red, and Chris Staples was standing near Frank glaring at him so fiercely I thought I would see two holes burn into Frank's skull."

Robertson addresses some of the traits for which Palmer is well known, such as his generosity. "He's generous today, but it would surprise a lot of outsiders to know that for a long time Frank was cheap, both financially and emotionally. Between his second and third wife, he was cheap with a lot of his girlfriends. If you took a sick day off, he berated you. Somewhere along the line he changed, but it was a slow transformation into the generous Frank Palmer everyone knows today."

Was it maturity that caused the change? Robertson smiles at the unlikely thought. "Doubt it. Perhaps Marika nagged him into changing, and if so, good for her. But to be fair, he became very financially well off in the late 1990s, and he has a natural proclivity to share."

Robertson says of all the achievements she witnessed during her tenure, Palmer was most proud of *Strategy* magazine ranking Palmer Jarvis as Canada's most creative agency. "That was huge not only for us, but for the Vancouver ad industry overall. Right up there too in terms of career highs was Frank winning the Entrepreneur of the Year Award; that appealed enormously to his business side."

Unfortunately, the lows were equally memorable. "Without a doubt, losing the McDonald's account and having to let staff go was horrible," says Robertson. "A lot of people don't realize that Frank's obsession with winning is not just about him winning; it's about him and everyone under his wing winning. So when he lost McDonald's he felt as if he'd let his staff down. He took his duties as an employer very seriously, and was unrelenting about making sure that talented and hard-working people were treated well. So having to let some of them go was excruciating for him to deal with."

It should be noted that Palmer's fairness as an employer is such that during Robertson's tenure and beyond, no employee ever took him to court. "In some cases, staff members who had been fired would even be rehired years later," says Robertson. "For all his talk about getting revenge on people, Frank never burned any bridges. When Chris Staples left Palmer Jarvis and took key personnel with him to form his own agency, Frank told me, 'I was a young guy once and would have done exactly the same thing.'"

*   *   *

Robertson's reference to Staples triggers a new line of storytelling, about a subject that changed Palmer Jarvis and Palmer forever, transformed him into a national advertising force and cemented his name for the ages—at least in industry circles.

Palmer had decided that the only way his twelve-partner agency could survive and grow further was to join a giant based in New York. In November 1997, he and DDB senior vice president John Bradstock made a deal for stock in Omnicom, which owned DDB. Under the deal, Palmer Jarvis would merge with the Toronto subsidiary of DDB Needham Worldwide to become Palmer Jarvis DDB.

In terms of Palmer's business prowess it was the deal to end all deals. Overnight it turned a highly regarded Western Canadian agency into one that could service international accounts—which Palmer viewed as vital to survival in the twenty-first century.

Ron Woodall notes that DDB also benefited substantially from the liaison. "For a very long time before the merger, DDB's Toronto office had been struggling and losing money," he says. "Keith Reinhard's concept was that the Vancouver culture should infect and direct Toronto so that eventually there would be product parity, enabling the agency to be a creative powerhouse nationally."

In terms of timing, the deal couldn't have been more apt. At the brink of the new millennium Vancouver was all grown up—at least on the outside. But the glittering towers of the re-developed False Creek and other areas of the downtown core couldn't disguise the fact that, despite decades of aggressive growth, the city's home-grown businesses were more than ever susceptible to takeovers. Despite lip service paid to "proudly local," nobody beyond entrepreneurs themselves seemed interested in encouraging substantial growth of local business; this attitude helped make everyone from grocers to architects ripe for purchase by larger foreign interests. Palmer, at least, was going to ensure that the purchase of his agency met all of his criteria, not someone else's.

The DDB deal capped three years of Palmer quietly negotiating with potential buyers and then turning down offers on the grounds he was being treated discourteously and disrespectfully. "The one thing I gained from that long courtship was the ability to say 'fuck you' way more easily than I'd ever done before, and I was hardly a shrinking violet before then," he says.

Palmer's decision to sell was a huge about-face—but entirely justified from his viewpoint, considering the evolving dynamics of the ad world. "The business was changing fundamentally, and very quickly, and I had no intention of not staying on top of the situation," he says. "By the early 1990s there were only two or three Canadian companies still doing business, all of them located in Toronto and little more than branches of multinationals headquartered in New York or England."

Despite Palmer's decades of hard work and the remarkable legacy he'd established, the DDB deal was an absolute necessity moving forward. "We didn't have the resources of these multinationals, so we needed DDB," he says. "Fortunately, the deal was structured so that decisions could be made by me right here in Vancouver, which was beneficial to clients."

As for the future, Palmer correctly predicted in a 1994 *Strategy* interview that "I think we'll see either some very good small boutique agencies, and some fairly large agencies, but the mid-sized agencies will either merge or go out of business."

Palmer's turnabout bewildered many of his staff, but not ob-servers like Red Robinson. "Frank always looks toward the future as a pragmatist, so instead of running the risk of eventually going out of business, he decided to sell," he says. "Fortunately for every-one involved, he was scrupulous about selling to the right people. There's no question in my mind that he didn't want to give up the company he'd built, but it would ensure that his team would keep their jobs for decades to come."

Chris Staples disagrees. With a laugh and a wave of his hand, he dismisses any notion that Palmer was being altruistic. "The creative revitalization of Palmer Jarvis gave him the respect he craved from the ad world, and now he wanted the money to go along with it," he says. "The fact of the matter is he loved to buy houses, go on trips and drive fancy cars, and therefore he was always short of cash. As a man in his fifties still haunted by the idea he could wind up on the skids, he wanted security. And he got it with DDB: the sale of his agency was in the double-digit millions."

*   *   *

The day the agency was signed over to DDB, Palmer nearly had a meltdown, not because of what the signing signified but because of the people involved. "It took place in our boardroom, and our twenty-five-foot-long table was covered with legal documents," he recalls. "There was even more paperwork balanced on the win-dow ledge that ran the length of the boardroom, and still more documents attached to the walls. The adjoining room was filled with legal papers too."

Palmer and eleven partners (three from Edmonton, four from Winnipeg, four from Vancouver) were charged with signing over the company. "The problem was that some of those partners decided to cause me grief by holding out at the last minute," he says. "Colin Ferguson, who had only a 2 per cent share in the company, gave me the most headaches, followed by Roald Thomas with a 17 per cent share. Neither of them thought they were getting enough money out of the deal, and at one point the arguing between us got so bad that I went into my office and screamed at the ceiling."

Chris Staples sympathizes. "To be honest, I regarded Frank's partners as a high-maintenance bunch of drama queens who didn't add much to the business."

Having vented his inner demons, Palmer re-emerged from his office with an ultimatum for his colleagues. "I told them they didn't need to sign, but if they didn't they wouldn't be working for me afterwards," he says. "They were appalled. They said, 'You can't do that,' and I replied, 'Just watch me.'"

So, standing in front of teams of lawyers, the partners picked up Montblanc pens that had been purchased for the occasion and signed Palmer Jarvis away. "When it came my turn to sign the final document, my energy level plummeted from an unbelievable high into a funk with a single stroke of the pen," says Palmer. "I went home and got drunk—really drunk. The following morning I went to work as if nothing had happened." Palmer was now president and CEO of Palmer Jarvis DDB (soon to be DDB Canada), and the head office was now in Vancouver, not Toronto.

Suddenly the door was open to national and international assignments, and within a year Palmer Jarvis DDB employed 375 people and reported fees approaching $36 million. The client roster ranged from smaller western accounts (including Playland, Richmond Savings Credit Union and TV12) to national advertisers such as Lever Pond's, Compaq Canada and Clorox Company of Canada.

Ron Woodall points out that Palmer Jarvis DDB maintained its reputation as an awards juggernaut. "By the end of the first year with DDB, *Marketing* magazine identified us as the agency winning the most new business in Canada. In 1999 we were named Canada's Agency of the Year by *Marketing*. This would be the first of three consecutive wins, the first triple ever. In 2000 we were named Canada's Agency of the Year by both *Strategy* magazine and the *National Post*."

Woodall adds, "It's worth noting that this success was all the more remarkable considering Palmer Jarvis got the momentum rolling in a regional market so small that except for a rare federal government assignment, there was not one national account to be had."

To the press, Palmer remained gung-ho about the sale to DDB, and at one point he told reporters that management had successfully transfused the Palmer Jarvis culture and values into the Toronto operation. "I spend two weeks a month in Toronto now, and I feel as much at home here as I do in Vancouver," he told the eastern press. "Walking into this office, the chemistry and enthusiasm is the same as in Vancouver. There's the same teamwork, integrity and passion to win."

The Palmer Jarvis staff also retained their ability to enjoy themselves after hours. "The annual Christmas parties were the stuff of legend, and for one of them Frank organized the event to take place at a well-known local restaurant," says Hugh Ruthven. "Before it began, Frank took the owner aside and said, 'I just need to remind you that these guys drink a lot.' The owner replied, 'Yes, I know.' Frank said, 'You don't understand, I'm telling you these guys drink *a lot*.' The owner got mad: 'I realize that, Frank. Don't tell me how to do my business.'

"So the party started at eight with 120 people attending. By the time it was getting into full swing around eleven, the owner realized his entire establishment had been drunk dry and everyone was demanding more. It wasn't uncommon after these events for Frank to be handed a bar tab of $40,000."

On the business side of things, the national brand work earned Palmer and his colleagues one of their most prestigious honours. At the 1999 Cannes advertising awards, Palmer Jarvis DDB won a Gold Lion for a TV spot done on behalf of Finesse Shampoo from Lever Pond's. It was the first Gold Lion a Canadian agency had brought home from Cannes in a decade.

At a time when even the cleverest of ads rarely make a lasting impression, the Finesse ad is still fondly remembered. In it, a man reads a shockingly bad poem about his wife: "Your hair is your best feature because it's more or less the colour of my workbench." Finesse's Canadian sales had been moribund prior to the ad; afterward, they increased by 15 per cent.

DDB made Palmer wealthy. Instead of a cash settlement, he accepted Omnicom stock at $38 per share, with a sixty-day no-divest period. Palmer referred to the agreement as "somewhat like putting your entire life's savings on the craps table in Las Vegas." His partners also accepted stock as part of the buyout.

In the ensuing months Omnicom stock fell and then rose. Palmer's partners ultimately sold their shares for their original value, but Palmer waited for a year and sold for $65–$70 per share.

Purely in terms of numbers, the sale was a source of pride for Palmer, who forever after would talk about it to friends in a tone containing a measure of wonder. "I basically sold Palmer

Jarvis for $10 million in stock that was worth $37 per share at the time and waited until the shares' worth doubled," he says. "In today's finances, the transaction wouldn't be worth $20 million, it would be $100 million. So just in terms of numbers, the sale was a white-hot success."

Alan Gee, who was based in Toronto and up until that point had only rubbed shoulders with Palmer at industry events, became better acquainted with him following the merger. "I'll never forget sitting with him in the Carlton Hotel in Cannes," he says. "He laid out every detail of the deal he'd made with DDB, including how much stock he got. I was flabbergasted, because in this business people tell you half of what you need to know, and usually that half turns out to be total bullshit. And yet here we were, both competing for the Gold Lion, and Frank was being as candid as if I were his long-lost brother."

Palmer was still the same old Frank, and his approach to business was intact, but his agency had changed profoundly. Staples says, "When we were first told that Palmer Jarvis would be sold, my immediate reaction was positive because DDB people like Bernbach were giants in the ad world, truly inspirational." Staples is referring to William Bernbach, whose towering achievements in the ad world included giving the Volkswagen Beetle a loveable, anti-establishment personality in 1960; prior to his intervention it had been considered a vaguely ugly if efficient product of German manufacturing.

But Staples's admiration for DDB was tempered by bitterness. "My partners and I had doubled the worth of Palmer Jarvis, and here we were having the rug pulled out from under us," he explains.

Staples remained with Palmer Jarvis DDB for a little more than a year, during which time his admiration for DDB wore off completely.

"The minute the company owned Frank, instead of reporting to him we were reporting to accountants in New York," he says.

Palmer doesn't complain about New York's influence except when well and truly riled. However, the satisfaction he got from the Palmer Jarvis sale began to erode early on too, when he spent time at Palmer Jarvis DDB's Toronto office. "Whenever I went to that city, which was frequently, I was treated like an outcast, as if I were a small Vancouver player who had merely lucked out," he says. "More to the point, everyone in that office ran around busily and importantly, but pretty soon I discovered they were in actuality losing a fortune due to mismanagement. I was furious—how dare they treat me as if I were a second-class citizen when they couldn't even do their own jobs effectively?"

Palmer endured six months of being made to feel second-rate until he finally lost his temper and lowered the boom. He called all the senior executives into his office and informed them, "The agency's name is Palmer Jarvis DDB, not DDB Palmer Jarvis. Furthermore, you're a bunch of fucking losers running around with your noses in the air, not even realizing you're frittering away $3 million annually."

The stunned group simply stood there, open-mouthed. With the veins standing out on his head, Palmer added, "Well, all this is about to change, as of this minute."

The executives had heard of Palmer's ruthlessness but figured they were in store for a milquetoast, West Coast form of bluster at best. They were ill-prepared for what happened next: Palmer went on a firing spree, with the president being the biggest casualty. Palmer then hired Jim Hurler to run the Toronto office and subsequently recruited other Vancouver talent to fill the shoes of Toronto upper management.

DDB took note and asked Palmer to clean up other offices. "Basically they gave me a lot of shit to clean up, and I'm still doing it," he says. Within three years, Palmer was also named president and CEO of DDB Group Canada.

Palmer's acquisition of new talent included hiring Kevin Brady in 1999 as president of the Anderson agency (later Anderson DDB Health & Lifestyle) in Toronto, which at the time "was $2 million in the hole," according to Brady, now 63.

Brady, who had worked at J. Walter Thompson and had been president of The Gingko Group, recalls Palmer taking him to dinner at the Hyatt Plaza Hotel in order to determine his professional mettle. "He asked me how I deal with stress, and I told him I was like the character Robert Duvall played in *Apocalypse Now*, striding along calmly as bombs are going off all around him," he says. "Bombs are going off constantly in the advertising business: you have to choose which ones you deal with. Frank liked that analogy."

Over the course of a year Brady turned Anderson into an agency that earned $7 million in revenue, and subsequently he became part of Palmer's inner circle, travelling to various destinations for business and pleasure.

Palmer's trajectory was so propulsive that it took him a while to fully appreciate the changes in his life. More attuned was Marika, who refers to the Palmer Jarvis sale as "the day everything changed for us. It seemed that Frank was constantly on the road and I was left alone. I'm trying not to complain, because materially I have absolutely nothing to complain about. But it was tough being without Frank, and I started to fantasize about a time when he would begin to slow down, perhaps spend half the year in Palm Springs just painting—which is the most romantic aspect about him—and the other six months here taking care of business. I still have that fantasy; we talk about it all the time. Or maybe I should say, I talk about it to him all the time."

Palmer's comeback is predictable. "Marika is always getting at me to spend more time with her. She would love nothing better than for me to retire, which I could easily do from a financial standpoint. But doing nothing would kill me. Even when I break down and agree to spend evenings watching TV with her, I can't seem to pay much attention to the screen—I'm too busy thinking about other things."

Marika found herself in a Catch-22, partly of her own making. The older Palmer got, the more she indulged her obsession of keeping him fit. The fitter he became, the more endurance he had for going on the road. "Frank has had health scares several times throughout our marriage, but he's always bounced back," she says.

As monolithic and ominous as some people regarded DDB, its no-nonsense CFO, Keith Bremer, can be credited for achieving the nearly impossible: pulling the wool over Palmer's eyes. He recalls, "During a trip to New York he planted one of those stupid devices in my production assistant's office where it was making cricket noises, and she got so upset trying to find the thing that she was threatening to cut off Frank's balls—so I decided to play a gag on him."

Waiting until Palmer and Marika flew to Cannes for a vacation, Bremer contacted the building manager of the DDB Vancouver headquarters and paid him $5,000 to remove the door to Palmer's office and have the opening drywalled to match the rest of the corridor.

A week later Palmer strolled down the corridor with his door key in hand, only to find a smooth wall adorned with a single framed painting. Baffled, he wondered if someone had the temerity to move his office, but a quick inspection proved this theory incorrect. Adding to his quickly mounting outrage was the fact that staff either didn't seem to know what had happened or were unwilling to talk.

Bremer's hard, clipped, New York–style way of talking tightens even more with amusement as he picks up the story. "At one point Frank walked out of the building and looked up to the spot where his office was, and sure enough he could still see his desk and bookshelves—and at that point he realized he'd been had, and by whom."

Palmer lost no time contacting Bremer long distance. "Very funny. When are you going to put my fucking door back on so I can get into my own office?"

"I have no idea what you're talking about, Frank."

Envisioning the amount of work piling up in his computer on the other side of the wall, Palmer panicked. "How am I supposed to get things done around here without an office?"

Bremer replied, "The way I see it, you have two options: you can either use the boardroom, or you can take up residence in one of the washroom stalls. Take your pick." And he hung up.

Bremer would later tell colleagues, "I let him sweat for a few days and then got the building manager to take down the drywall and remount the door. It felt great getting the better of Frank: you have to watch yourself even if you go to dinner with him, and God help you if you leave the table to go to the bathroom, because sure as hell he'll empty the salt shaker into your coffee or stuff a pastry into your jacket pocket."

Bremer wasn't finished with Palmer: waiting until his colleague embarked on another overseas trip, he got workers to strip Palmer's office bare and install a water fountain in the middle. Palmer recalls, "When I came back, the place looked like some phony tropical island resort, like you would see in the display window of a department store."

He smiles at the memory. "Maybe those were the last of the good old days in terms of pulling out all the stops to perpetrate a good gag. I can't imagine executives of today spending more than five cents to play a joke on someone—not that they would be inclined to play jokes at all."

Although Palmer felt contractually and morally obligated to stay for the long haul at Palmer Jarvis DDB, Chris Staples did not. In 1999 he, Tom Shepansky and Ian Grais decided to strike out on their own and form Rethink Communications. "I was enormously respectful of Frank but couldn't stand being an anonymous branch of a New York company anymore," he says. "We kept our plans for Rethink a secret, but the actual split from DDB turned out to be awful. That's because Hugh Ruthven initially wanted to fall in with us, but after we agreed to each put up $25,000 in order to launch Rethink, he got cold feet, backed out and told Frank what was going on."

Staples was astonished when he and his colleagues were still invited to attend a big planning meeting the following morning. There, faced with Palmer and other DDB personnel, Staples launched into a rant about how New York had decreed that every photocopy machine be operated with a punch-in code, which enabled the head office to bill clients for the photocopies. "That's exactly the kind of nonsense that's causing us to leave!" he hollered.

Palmer remembers the diatribe. "I wasn't impressed," he says. "I'm no defender of bureaucracy or penny-pinching, but I didn't see anything wrong with the way the photocopiers operated, for God's sake; the punch-in codes prevented staff from copying reams and reams of stuff that had nothing to do with work."

Because Staples was widely viewed in media circles as the catalyst for Palmer Jarvis's resurrection, word quickly spread that his departure would be a blow from which Palmer would never recover. "And to our discredit, we too were convinced the agency would collapse," says Staples. "Mark it down to the arrogance of youth."

Palmer admitted to journalist David Todd at the time that "It definitely hurts when you lose someone valued like that. But then you get over it, and you move on. I'm a survivor."

However, he laughed off the prognostication of his professional demise. "At no point did I take the rumours seriously," he recalls. "Sure, I was going to miss Chris; but I was also of the firm opinion that change brings opportunity, and when someone leaves an organization it gives other people in that organization the chance to grow—or it attracts new blood."

Less than a month after losing Staples and other staff, Palmer Jarvis DDB won a $10-million Budweiser account from Labatt Breweries of Canada. Many years later after steady growth, DDB Canada would bill a total of $800 million for 2009, at a time when industry-wide performance was declining in the double digits. As the parent firm's Canadian marketplace operator, Palmer was also running its health-and-lifestyle agency Anderson DDB, which was based in Montreal and in 2009 was billing in the $100-million range.

Nobody is more impressed with this performance than Staples. "It could be argued that our departure gave Frank a kick in the pants, a new enemy," he muses. "It also allowed new talent to come into his agency, and in short order he exceeded what we had achieved in the 1990s by far."

But Staples's mindset was different back then, and the early success of Rethink prompted a rivalry between him and Palmer, the tone and timbre of which embarrass him today. "We both said stupid things to the media, me especially," he recalls. "I would brag openly about taking the Playland account from Frank and declaring that it would cause his business to collapse. So stupid. Three years elapsed before we had lunch together, and from that point we became friendly competitors."

Palmer exhibits undisguised pride when asked to discuss life after Staples's departure from the company in 1999. "Chris leaving with Shepansky and Grais put me in a spot, no doubt about it. But we didn't go backwards as everyone predicted. In a very real sense, the collective talent at Palmer Jarvis is far stronger than that of any individual or small group of individuals."

The excitement of landing major contracts compensated for many shortcomings. One of the more fulfilling contracts for Palmer was for the Canadian Tourism Commission (CTC), which he won in 2001 by pitching under the umbrella support of DDB Worldwide. The business would be worth billings of $4 million to $5 million annually, making the CTC the Vancouver agency's most valuable client in terms of revenue.

CTC interim CEO Greg Klassen was then a newcomer in charge of the CTC's e-marketing section. "You've heard this before many times, but DDB's pitch blew the competition right out of the water, which in our case was no mean feat because there were many competitors closely aligned with government, plus it's very difficult to win our business," he says. "DDB simply did their homework, had great ideas and presented very well."

The fact that Palmer later left a phone message with each and every CTC staff member was a personal thrill for Klassen. "I couldn't believe Frank Palmer had taken the time to leave someone like me, who was young and green, a phone message stating how excited he was to represent the CTC and how hard he was going to work on our behalf," he recalls. "I wound up saving that message and kept replaying it. A class act."

Few if any clients work with Palmer without experiencing a "Frankism" or two, and Klassen is no exception. "We undertake an agency review about every five years, and when DDB re-pitched to us in 2006 we deliberately limited the number of people who did the pitch to those who would actually be working on the business—which meant we had four DDB people in the room and not Frank, who was too busy overseeing his company's operations. However, he got around our regulations anyway by videotaping a presentation and having his team play it during a crucial point in their pitch!"

Now as the ambassador to an entire country, DDB was tasked with making Canada the go-to destination for vacationers around the world. The cumulative efforts of the agency are remarkable. Palmer notes, "We turned Canada from being the sixty-seventh best place to visit in the world to fifth, to second and finally to first. In 2012 we became second again, but only because the CTC didn't spend so much money on promotions."

DDB helped rocket Canada into the stratosphere of tourism by devising ad campaigns that were "more than just Mounties and maple syrup," according to Palmer. "Our programs, under the brand 'Canada Keep Exploring,' highlighted Canadians exploring their country in a multitude of different ways. We produced snippets of commercials rather than full commercials, and we developed a presence on YouTube for the CTC that really generated a lot of interest."

Palmer's description doesn't do justice to the multi-year campaign that actually transpired. Klassen says, "In 2006 they gave a powerful pitch that focused on using social media at a time when Facebook was only a few years old. I can't stress enough how revolutionary this was, and it also solved a problem we had regarding having a limited budget but seeking maximum exposure."

Klassen also singles out DDB Canada's Cosmo Campbell, who in 2017 is senior vice president and chief creative officer, for taking a radically different approach to the conventional ad agency method of shooting video commercials. "He came up with the idea of turning the camera over to everyday Canadians," he says. "You have to understand that video production is a huge revenue source for ad agencies, but DDB forwent this revenue stream because it was too good an idea to pass up. We spread the message via social media that we wanted Canadians to take their own cameras and promote Canada the way they saw fit, and as a result we wound up with thousands of hours' worth of footage that was eventually trimmed down to two commercials, one running two minutes, the other thirty seconds."

According to the *Huffington Post*, DDB's handiwork (or more accurately, the handiwork of Canadians) became the second most viewed video of all time, anywhere. "We put the commercials into theatres in the UK, and patrons reportedly went to the theatre managers asking them to run the spots again," says Klassen.

On November 26, 2012, Klassen emailed Palmer and his team, congratulating them on their success:

I wanted to email you specifically to thank you and your team for your support, enthusiasm and even risk for our highly successful $35-million directors' campaign. I know that as agency professionals, you are accustomed to fading to the background to allow the client to step up and take the credit, but today I want to thank you and your team for your huge contribution to this outcome.

As you know, this program, like many others we have done together, didn't fit neatly inside any kind of marketing box.

In addition to our primary objective of creating an anthem for Canada that would inspire and compel visitors from around the world to choose Canada, our other objective included engaging Canadians in the great work that we do at the CTC and in turn supporting a tourism industry integral to so many communities across Canada. Before I explain exactly how you over-delivered on the second objective, let me tell you of a handful of early wins in less than a week of launch:

- Six days in, and almost 250K YouTube hits. I can't recall any other CTC communications effort that gained so much traction in such a short period of time.
- By Friday, after three days of launch on movie screens in the UK, we received 121K views on our website . . . and there's four weeks to go in that campaign.
- In Japan we received 10K likes . . . way more likes than we even have of Facebook fans.
- On our Keep Exploring Facebook page we have 4,446 shares and 6,715 likes.
- We have had media pick-up from across Canada and around the world with super-positive commentary from Fast Company to George

Strombo to Huffington Post, to some of the coolest
bloggers and media personalities around.

- We have had a request from the National Capital
Commission to play the video on the main stage at
Canada Day in 2013 in Ottawa.
- We have had a request from our International Trade
Partners in India and Ottawa to use the video to
introduce Canada at their events.
- We have the Weather Network asking to run it
throughout their programming.
- We debuted the video at TIAC's Tourism Awards
Gala with 50 MPS and senators in attendance to
rousing applause.
- The comments, messages and kudos keep coming
in . . . many, many more examples to come in the
weeks ahead.

So it's clear based on early indicators that this video
will accomplish our primary objective. The world is in love
with Canada, and our new anthem just may be the glue
to inspire people to visit us in a year where our traditional
marketing dollars will be more limited than ever. Thank
you for your contribution to this important outcome . . .
But what I'm really writing about is to thank you for
your contribution to the second objective of engaging
Canadians, where ddb did more. You proved that you put
your customers first.

✳   ✳   ✳

Ron Woodall's one regret about the myriad changes occurring at DDB Canada was that "with the yearly staff turnover, fewer and fewer people, perhaps not one in ten, were here to experience the cultural evolution. The other nine had little idea of how the morphing unfolded. What they did know is that they joined the team that was always ranked number one. For these people, perhaps there was less passion to excel. Perhaps they needed to understand the original vision and the process of change. The concept of being unique, respected and a leader should be kept alive in a very meaningful sense."

The continued upward trajectory of Palmer's agency didn't detract from the fact that Palmer was sitting somewhat awkwardly in the midst of a new era of advertising—an era dominated by suits with no skin in the game.

His bosses viewed him as a valued senior statesman, which he regarded with profound ambivalence. On one hand, it was an undeniable show of respect. On the other, it bothered the twenty-year-old in Palmer. In this context, some of his upbeat comments to the press in the early years of the DDB era seem ironic; for example, the frequently repeated quote, "I'm the chief cheerleader. I don't have the pompoms, but I'm there cheering for the team, giving high fives and celebrating wins."

As team-oriented as Palmer is, he hardly fits the role of a cheerleader spurring others on from the sidelines. In fact, the older Palmer gets, the more his intervention helps bring ad campaigns to successful fruition.

Dean Mailey points out that Palmer "gets frustrated with people who display attitude, and in this age of social media there are no end of younger folk who think they know everything, especially in the ad world. The source of his frustration is that these same people really don't understand why companies succeed or fail, because they're too busy being right and hip."

On one occasion Jim Pattison retained Palmer's team to design a logo for the now defunct AirWest passenger carrier that would be displayed on the tails of the company jets. Pattison requested a stylized *A* for the design; the team created several dozen variations, and Palmer displayed them all in Pattison's boardroom. After several minutes of study, Pattison said, "Give it another shot. What I'd really like to see is the letter *A* on the tails of my jets."

The team returned to the drawing boards and produced more variations, which were displayed in Pattison's boardroom. Pattison studied them and told Palmer, "You're making some headway, but once again I'd still like to see an *A* on the tails of my jets."

Incensed by his colleagues, Palmer took it upon himself to fulfill Pattison's request. At his drawing board early next morning he produced two designs with a distinct *A* and then resumed his other duties. When one of the younger team members visited him later that day, he remarked about how relaxed Palmer seemed. "I am," Palmer replied. "Because I just did what all of you guys failed to do."

Later that day the team returned to Pattison's boardroom and unveiled their latest series of designs, including Palmer's handiwork. Within seconds, Palmer's two designs were singled out as the winning contenders. "Two months later the two guys who had been designing things for me quit," Palmer recalls. "The point is that you can't sell things you think the client should have; you can only sell what the client wants."

If Palmer was caught in a transitional world, saddled with the unsettling mantle of elder statesman, at least there were elements of the old style of business that would probably never go away: the uniquely odd allegiances that formed under the most unlikely of circumstances, fuelled as much by skulduggery as by a compulsion for friendship.

Palmer fondly recalls John Hayter, who became president and CEO of Vickers & Benson in 1990 and presided over a portfolio that included Bank of Montreal, Cantel, CFTO-TV, Ford, M&M Meats and McDonald's. "During that time he had McDonald's in Ontario and we had McDonald's in Western Canada, we decided to meet," he says. "So John took the red-eye to Vancouver, came into my office and immediately after shaking my hand, stretched out on my couch as if he were going to bed. It wasn't exactly love at first sight, but we connected immediately, and we talked about everything from our kids to how to get more business out of McDonald's. It was the start of a long friendship."

The friendship, of course, overflowed with classic ad-man moments, such as the time Hayter asked Palmer to come to a party in Toronto because there was a beautiful girl he wanted Palmer to meet. "So I dressed casually with the intent of looking very hip, and sure enough, early on in the party this girl came over to me and started chatting," says Palmer. "She was gorgeous, things were going great, and just as I was about to make my move John comes over and asks, 'How do you like my new girlfriend?' All my notions of being hip and suave were swept away as if by a windshield wiper."

By the time the DDB era arrived, Palmer was well-accustomed to Hayter's peccadilloes. "He could be like the Tasmanian devil when drunk, and one time after knocking back a few he stood on a bar top, did a backflip and landed on his heels instead of the balls of his feet," says Palmer. "He hobbled into a meeting the next day in excruciating pain, and I don't think he ever fully recovered from the injury."

Palmer recounts this particular incident because one night he found himself drinking with Hayter at a Hyatt watering hole. "John was in a foul mood, and what we didn't know about each other was that I was looking to hire a new president to run DDB and he was looking for a new man to run Vickers—and that he was courting my guy Dave Leonard and I was courting his senior executives! And sure as hell, I wound up hiring his man Tony Alitilia, and John wound up hiring Leonard.

"Here we were, best of friends, but never telling each other about what was going on until the hiring had been completed."

More intrigue, albeit with a less humorous outcome, followed. It eventually became apparent that Alitilia wasn't working out for Palmer, and over in Hayter's corner Leonard made it known to a search consultant that he wanted to return to DDB. The timing was good because Palmer wanted to replace Jim Hurler in the Toronto office, so he quickly negotiated to make Leonard his replacement. "I then went down to Cabo San Lucas with Marika and John for a quick vacation, and upon our return John learned about Dave rejoining DDB," says Palmer. "He went ballistic and accused me of being a prick—not so much because Dave left his fold, but because he thought I'd taken him to Cabo solely to get him away from the office so I could do some manoeuvring. Which wasn't the case at all."

Palmer smiles somewhat sadly and shakes his head. "Only in the advertising world. John hasn't spoken to me since, and I miss his company."

The bad news wasn't over yet. "Jim Hurler accused me of putting a fifty-five-year-old man—meaning him—on the street," says Palmer. "But the fact of the matter is that after he left DDB he travelled the world with his wife, so in my mind maybe he should thank me! Today he suffers me in small doses, which is better than nothing. I really like the guy."

* * *

In 2010, after almost twenty-two years of service, Hilary Robertson resigned as Palmer's personal assistant. There had been no fight, no brewing bad feelings, no lack of enthusiasm for the job.

Instead, Robertson had become increasingly disenchanted with the DDB culture. "During my last few years, Frank and I felt the influence of DDB in a way we didn't enjoy," she says. "New York was becoming very heavy handed."

Robertson says that although the Vancouver headquarters of DDB Canada enjoyed a stellar creative reputation within the organization, at the end of the day the policy makers were interested only in a return on their investment. "When the recession of 2008 hit they really started twisting the thumbscrews," she recalls. "Every year we had to go to New York and present our numbers to the big brass, and every year there would be budget slashes and layoffs."

Although fully aware that bottom lines had to be maintained, Robertson describes the financial pressure everyone had to endure as "dreadful. To make matters worse, New York's creeping fingers were getting into everything. Today, nobody in Vancouver can do anything without getting New York's approval."

As the pressures mounted, Robertson found herself being increasingly protected by Palmer. "He carried the pressure and let me get on with my job. At one point, to save money, New York slashed my Christmas bonus by two-thirds. When Frank found out about this, he paid me the two-thirds out of his own bonus—and the amount was substantial."

Her voice tightening slightly, Robertson goes on to describe the end. "I carried on for a while, but Frank realized that if he left DDB or retired before I did, there would be no way New York would give me a fair severance. I would be nickelled and dimed to death. So one day he said, 'I'll fire you, and that way I can ensure you get a good severance.' And I thought, 'Thank you, Jesus.' Incidentally, I wasn't the only person he did this for."

A few weeks prior to Robertson's departure, Palmer honoured her by booking the private wine room at Umberto's and hosting a dinner for her and twenty colleagues. He also gave her a $5,000 travel voucher, and the company awarded her with a TAG Heuer wristwatch for her long service.

Robertson's last day on the job was December 24, 2010; goodbyes had been exchanged with colleagues earlier, so her only task was to clean out her desk. To her dismay, Palmer left the office without saying goodbye at all. She recalls, "I later sent him an email asking why, and he replied that it would have been too hard for him to say goodbye in person."

I was reading an article about how many people spend a great deal of their lives working and living in a comfort zone. A comfort zone is inextricably linked to habits, like using the same route to go to work every day, or having fish and chips every Friday.

The trouble is, comfort zones aren't necessarily good. Take going to the gym. Many people who do the same routine every day see no substantial gain for their efforts. That's because in order for their bodies to lose fat or gain muscle, they need to be shocked by doing different exercises on different days.

Look, I know it's easier to be comfortable than to stretch yourself. When a rubber band is relaxed it takes no energy to stay that way, but when you stretch it, it takes energy to hold it flexed. But you'll get nowhere in life without flexing or stretching.

The one piece of advice that I can share with you is that it's never too late to start to do something different.

The article I was reading went on to state that old people rarely regret what they've done in their life, but they *do* regret what they haven't done. I think that should also apply to younger people.

I never ever want to have to say that I wanted to do something different but never found the time to do so. I want to be able to say that I tried, did my best or gave it a good shot.

Don't sit on the sidelines and watch the opportunities in life go to the ones who flexed and stretched themselves.

— FRANK PALMER

Turmoil, Transformation and *Real Housewives*

I n 2013, Bob Stamnes came across an *Esquire* magazine story that caused his heart to pound, and he promptly emailed it to as many friends and colleagues as possible, stating, "A great article—my sentiments exactly. Incredibly bang on."

He also emailed it to Palmer, who was more and more pondering his future at DDB Canada and lamenting over the turn his industry had taken.

The story "Where Advertising Will Go Next" by David Droga, the renowned creative chairman of Droga5, was part of *Esquire*'s "Best and Brightest" series, and ran in the December 2013 issue.

Anyone who's ever failed to close a pop-up knows that advertising today is more about interruption and intrusion than compelling narratives or a good laugh. We don't add value. If anything, we often take it away.

But all that's going to change. Because it has to. Because it's harder than ever to hold anyone's attention for longer than a split second. Because mergers across our industry, like the one earlier this year between Publicis and Omnicom, are being done in the name of efficiency, not creativity. Because over the past fifteen years, many of those who get paid to practice what's considered the third-least-ethical profession in the country have gotten cynical in our thinking. In fact, no industry works harder at being lazy.

It's time advertising executives got the memo.

The introduction alone had gotten Stamnes's pulse racing, and it had the same effect on Palmer when he read the article. Droga was stating, in a revered mass-market magazine read around the world, what they and many other seasoned pros had been worrying about for some time now.

In the article, Droga wrote:

In the past, the size of an agency mattered. Big brands wouldn't even look at ad agencies unless they carried a big stick. But now, in an age when Netflix can win an Emmy, many clients are craving fresh thinking and output and finding them with smaller, more nimble agencies that are throwing themselves into uncharted waters to find new ways of doing things.

Panic buttons are being pressed at every legacy company around the world, and unless the Goliaths (like, say, the newly formed Publicis Omnicom Group) invest in research and development that will reinvent their business, they're going to continue trafficking in dead-end, middle-of-the-road output.

Now, a huge number of clients are happy with that approach, but they're fast becoming a minority. Creativity is a game changer. That's true of society, in advertising and in life. It's the daydreamers that change things, and today the little guys have the best chance of reaping the rewards.

Droga concluded that mobile advertising would be the advertising venue of the future—provided messages could be delivered in a non-intrusive and compelling manner.

In 2013, when he learned that Frank Palmer's biography was being written, Chris Staples also offered his opinion about how his industry was changing. It should be noted that nothing was particularly special about that year other than that big companies continued to get bigger through acquisitions, and social media (with Twitter only a few years old) was increasingly viewed as something that would soon fundamentally change the way people communicated and shared information.

Staples said, "This is either the best time in history to be in the ad business or the worst. On the one hand, there have never been more ways to engage with people about brands. In the old days, communication was one way, from brand to consumer. Now, through social media, it can be a true conversation. The internet also makes it much easier to find true believers in your brand and rally them. This is powerful stuff.

"On the other hand, all of the old ways of building brands are dying before our eyes. Nothing can replace the efficient emotional wallop of a well-done TV campaign. Social and digital media can build strong bonds, but they take much longer and cost much more relative to a quick hit on TV." He added, "As agencies, we need to find ways to create great content for less money. After all, the internet doesn't care about production gloss: just look at all those cat videos shot on iPhones."

For the old pros who left the industry before the big conglomerates grew bigger and before social media changed the world, a far more pleasing life awaited them. This was certainly true of George Jarvis, who by 2013 had become an increasingly hard man to pin down.

Jarvis was still doing a million things at once—but strictly on behalf of his family. At one point that year he took time out to travel to Burnaby and meet a friend at Brentwood Town Centre.

Jarvis was soft-spoken and his words were well considered. He bore none of the stereotypical traits of an ad man (or, to be more specific in his case, a former salesman): no quick talk, no flashy smile, no sense of having an underlying agenda. Only his gaze, which was sharp and somewhat uncomfortably probing, betrayed his long experience in an industry that seeks to influence decision making.

Jarvis's friend was intent on playing catch-up, to see what he thought of the industry he had gladly retired from. Jarvis, dressed in casual slacks and a short-sleeved shirt, made it clear that he was more interested in shopping for his grandkids than discussing business. But because the Sears outlet he was standing in front of hadn't yet opened, he and his friend sat down on a plastic bench; from his pocket Jarvis extracted a clipping of an article, by Susan

Krashinsky Robertson, from *The Globe and Mail*'s July 30, 2013 edition of *Report on Business*. The headline: "What's driving the ad world's global mega-merger: finance and ego."

"This," Jarvis informed his friend, waving the clipping, "is the end of our industry as we know it."

Robertson wrote that the planned merger between Omnicom Group Inc. and Publicis Groupe SA, which had been announced several days prior, would "reshape the industry landscape to create the world's biggest advertising agency holding company," bringing together a portfolio of creative agencies including BBDO, Leo Burnett, Saatchi & Saatchi and TBWA, and media buying and planning agencies such as OMD, Starcom and Zenith Optimedia, as well as public relations and digital agencies.

The deal was pitched as a way for the combined company to better compete in an age in which digital media, big data and a globally minded clientele had revolutionized the business. But Robertson noted that the birth of Publicis Omnicom Group came at a time "when advertising itself is changing rapidly, with marketing dollars flowing more and more into digital, and marketers are struggling to understand how to take advantage of technology to better compete for the attention, and wallets, of consumers."

With his gaze shifting from the clipping to the staff slowly gathering within Sears, Jarvis remarked that he wasn't so much interested in the particulars of the merger as he was in the bigger picture—and suddenly he asked his friend, who was a journalist, when he began his career.

"When I was a teenager," his friend said.

"So, before computers and cell phones?"

"Yep. We would hammer out our stories on electric typewriters and try to be as accurate as possible, because if you made a mistake you had to correct the mistake on the top paper as well as the two copies that were sandwiched between two sheets of carbon."

"So you understand where I'm coming from," Jarvis replied. "That wasn't so long ago, but you're a dinosaur. I'm a dinosaur too, and I'm glad of it. The industry has changed because the world has changed, but I honestly don't see the role of advertising in the future."

Jarvis let out a big sigh: not because he was longing for a simpler era, but because the Sears staff members were staging a group motivational meeting instead of opening the store on time. He continued: "We're living in an age when corporations know what our buying patterns and habits are, as well as our activities from one moment to the next. And this knowledge is becoming more and more focused. We're consuming information at a ferocious speed, and if advertising doesn't become obsolete, at least the delivery system will."

Finally, one of the Sears staff members walked over to the enormous glass and aluminum curtain separating eager mall shoppers from the products within, and pushed a button. The curtain rose, and so too did Jarvis's spirits. He folded the *Report on Business* clipping and smiled at the shoppers rushing past him. "I'm glad I'm where I am today, with my family enjoying old-fashioned face-to-face interaction," he said. "It was the personal relationships I developed during my time in the ad business that made that part of my life fun, but God knows what kind of industry advertising will evolve into."

Jarvis handed his friend the clipping as if it was the last remnant of his old life, and patted him on the shoulder. "Anyway, time to go. A few toys are in there that my grandkids have their eyes on." And he strolled happily toward the department store, not even glancing back once.

Another person happy to be free of the advertising business was Ron Woodall, who told a colleague: "When my father was alive, we would often visit him in Victoria. After dinner, we would watch TV. He would be in his big chair with his ten-foot bamboo pole duct-taped to the volume control to mute all commercials, mine and everyone else's. He had invented the remote. My father didn't believe that advertising was the most important thing in the whole world. Now, I have drifted over to his side."

Having become increasingly bear-like in appearance and now living full-time on Bowen Island as an informal resident artist, Woodall said, "I split my year between living on an island and living in Baja. It has been over ten years since I left DDB. Inexplicably, I immediately lost all interest in the agency and chose to have no further contact. So I have no sense of the business."

In fact, for years Woodall had been recognized as an artist, and his exhibitions prompted Sally Baker, gallery and cultural services manager for the Bowen Island Arts Council, to declare on the Bowen Online website, "His first love was always painting, and what he loved to paint most was the decaying architecture of ghost towns and abandoned places for which he has a passion."

She added that Woodall's watercolours, which had been exhibited in New York, would have easily impressed Robert Bateman or Andrew Wyeth.

Hugh Ruthven was another old pro who eventually found a more satisfying life away from the bustle of Metro Vancouver: he moved to Vancouver Island and became a brand planner for his own company, Intuition Brand Planning. "I left DDB because it was almost like working in a vacuum, going from pitch to pitch and feeding the lion," he said in 2013. "But Frank thrives on it, and his complete and total inability to recognize the passage of years can be galling. When I turned forty-one twelve years ago, he said to me, 'Well, you're on the back nine, aren't you.' The fucking audacity of the man, saying this when he was two decades older than me. I replied, 'Well, you're in the clubhouse and the lights are out.' He just laughed. To him, nothing could have been further from the truth."

But for every person who had left the industry or formed their own business, there was an equal number remaining who tried to predict what would happen next. Ryan Holiday, a best-selling author and advisor to many brands and writers, offered his thoughts in *The Observer*'s tech site, *BetaBeat*, in a 2013 story titled "Don Draper Is Dead: Why Growth Hack Marketing Is Advertising's Last Hope."

Holiday wrote that commercials, billboards and even online banners were rapidly becoming obsolete, at a time when most companies could arguably be thought of as tech companies:

> And this is the whole point. It took a group of geeks running tech companies—more in love with beautiful code than art projects or Times Square billboards—to see through the status quo and develop a new way. They had no patience for intangibles and gut instincts, so they developed an alternative.
>
> Let's face it. They beat us. So it's time to join 'em.

Even though Palmer had plenty of negative things to say about how the ad world had evolved and even worse things to say about younger people wasting their days peering at video screens ("I view social media as a platform enabling phony friends to spread gossip" was one of his more familiar declarations to friends and acquaintances), he also seemed entirely at home in the twenty-first century. Despite the stranglehold of technology, he still saw a world of humanity.

Shortly after he learned of Jarvis's opinion that traditional advertising was dead, Palmer sat down with a few colleagues in his office high above the law courts of downtown Vancouver and grinned. "Well, as far as mergers are concerned, they've been happening for years," he said. "It's commonplace in retail, in the auto industry, grocery, accounting firms, airlines—there isn't an industry that hasn't been affected by mergers."

The proposed Omnicom Group and Publicis Groupe merger was still making headlines, and Palmer had just finished talking to reporters and assuring his colleagues that everything would be okay, uttering soothing words in his silky voice about better economies of scale, improved efficiencies and cost savings. "Do I buy all that?" he said after ensuring that his office door was closed. "Yes, I do, but I also have no illusions that such mergers are really about big profits for very few people. Plus, no doubt it will be even harder for the small to mid-sized ad agencies to compete. Put it this way: I'd hate to start all over again with Trend Advertising in 2013."

Ron Woodall was expressing similar sentiments back in 2005. He wrote in his journal, "The Palmer Jarvis metamorphosis of 1993 probably could not happen now. To effect the change, there was a level of maverick underdog behaviour that would probably be unseemly in a multinational organization."

Woodall went on to note that Vancouver had become an increasingly difficult place to conduct business. "The list of failed West Coast agencies is long, and virtually every national account has now centralized and moved east: Nissan, Canadian Airlines, Japan Air, Safeway, Labatt Breweries, Hudson's Bay Company, Scott Paper, McDonald's, IKEA, Nabob and many others. That has choked off creative opportunities and forced whatever success we've had to become that much more of a scramble.

"Toronto suffers no such famine," Woodall continued. "Even if Vancouver retained its creative cachet, the department is always vulnerable as Toronto agencies can offer higher salaries and the opportunity to work on national accounts with much bigger budgets. Plus, newer, smaller, entrepreneurial shops in the east mimic the kind of independent culture that was once uniquely Palmer Jarvis's, but they do it in a much more fertile marketplace. Vancouver has become a tighter race and a harder recruit."

Palmer, having just defended big mergers publicly while admitting their devastating effect on small companies, ignored the dual interruption of his ringing desk phone and smart phone, and considered George Jarvis's other remarks. "I agree with him on a lot of points," he told his colleagues. "For one thing, I'm still here plugging away in an industry that is now run by accountants. Also, I'm not an owner anymore; I'm essentially a manager, but I still want to be an owner to this day, because I want control and there's still stuff I want to prove."

Palmer's daily thoughts were very much occupied by DDB, and from his perspective his relationship with the advertising giant was constantly being tested. "Keith Reinhard and Dick Rogers are still at DDB, and they're the guys who attracted me to the agency to begin with," he said. "But the company is no longer the family it once was, and in the past five or six years I've gotten a sense that the bosses want me more than ever—but at the same time they don't want me taking risks. All of a sudden they're treating us like bankers, trying to make us the same as every other ad person in the country."

Palmer found himself increasingly resisting head-office directives: "If we give in, we'll become just another anonymous agency."

Palmer made a few half-hearted attempts to quit DDB Canada, partly to gain enough free time to think clearly about what he wanted to do next: "I've stated on several occasions that I'll work half the time for half the pay, but the response is always the same: 'We'll still pay you in full.' When I ask why, they say, 'Because we know you'll never work only half the time.' And I guess they're right."

So Palmer stayed put, and the politics associated with his role as elder statesman compelled him to react in typically Palmerian ways. One morning his assistant, Veronica, walked into his office and dodged as a radio-controlled helicopter flew past her. Palmer was at the controls, seated at his desk, in a particularly foul mood after a two-hour long-distance battle concerning a new account.

"Everything okay?" Veronica asked as Palmer rotated in his chair to follow the path of the helicopter.

"You can't fit eighty pounds of shit into a ten-pound bag," he replied.

Having heard many variations of the same theme before, Veronica placed some folders on his desk, checked the trajectory of the helicopter and departed.

For many other professionals in their early seventies, ignoring something perceived to be broken is easy to do, if only because they have spent an entire career exposed to broken things. But anything imperfect to the often spectacularly imperfect Palmer irritated him like a hair shirt; like all true leaders, it wasn't about him, but about the company, and if something could be fixed, it was his duty to complain about it.

So rather than restrict his complaining to behind closed doors, he called attention publicly to problems whenever the opportunity arose. One venue was executive addresses. "The truth often hurts, and it's sometimes ugly, but anything less is a waste of time," he explains. "Relationships, and businesses, have never been improved by yes-men or people who can't bring themselves to say what they think."

Accordingly, Palmer's September 2013 speech to a handful of DDB executives at the Royal Vancouver Yacht Club quickly segued from a jovial beginning to his concerns about the future of his company.

He kicked off by noting that 15,856 days had elapsed since he entered the advertising industry in 1969, and he wished his audience the same longevity. He also congratulated them on a sterling 2012; he said, however, that "the problem is, we need to do even better this year" and "we now operate as three or four separate office teams."

As the executives shifted uncomfortably in their seats, Palmer continued: "What is our manifesto? We need to self-rate our work. Is it good enough? Can we do better? And where do we go from here? DDB North America wouldn't be all that happy with my remarks right now. They are working hard to fix a broken model. Mark O'Brien [president of DDB North America] has asked for my assistance, and frankly our Canadian model is a much better model."

Palmer was hardly finished baring his soul publicly. After reminding his audience how he had hired Ron Woodall to create a winning strategy for the firm he once owned, he said, "I'm really, really, really worried! Worried that, one, we are going to lose our entrepreneurial spirit. Two, that we are going to lose our feisty attitude. Three, that we aren't going to risk making fun of ourselves. And four, I'm really afraid of becoming just another corporate advertising agency.

"Are we being brave enough today or are we just comfortable? Are we the navy or are we still the pirates? DDB Canada has to date been successful, and to remain successful we are going to have to work harder and more differently than ever before. Our future brave actions will serve as the foundations that will move us from being good to being really great."

As much as Palmer was still gung-ho about taking care of everything when it came to handling clients, he was unable to violate personal principles, and on one occasion this caused him to lose a major account. The conflict began innocuously, with Palmer growing increasingly irritated by staff fiddling with their smart phones during board meetings.

At first, Palmer reprimanded them. "Would you mind putting those fucking things down and focusing on the business at hand?"

When the problem persisted, he augmented his reprimands by telling the culprits they would pay their own phone bills if the usage was for personal or entertainment purposes.

Before long, the local press published an item about Palmer's strategy to reduce cell phone usage, and Telus, which was one of his more valued clients, caught wind of the story. "Telus informed me I was being disrespectful to them and that it was my job to encourage people to use more airtime," he says. "We ultimately lost that account. But I couldn't help it: distracted attention is becoming a real disease, and something has to be done about it." It's interesting to note that Palmer was concerned about this several years before using a cell phone while driving became a criminal offence.

Palmer mitigated the frustration of his circumstances by trying to advance other people's careers. In 2010, with Canaccord Genuity vice president Mike Rogers, he founded the Palmer Rogers Encore Ventures firm in order to raise venture capital and provide marketing advice. "Mike and I welcome people through our doors and listen to their ideas, and if we like an idea in particular, we'll fund it on an OPM basis," said Palmer with a smirk. OPM is the abbreviation for Other People's Money.

This enterprise drew a significant number of colourful characters into Palmer's orbit. "This one guy, who had about as much hair as I do, had the nerve to come into my office trying to pitch a miracle hair restorer," Palmer recalled several years after the formation of Encore. "This is the kind of shit we find ourselves going through. Needless to say I turned him down, but awhile later he came back with a new gadget in the form of what looks like a metal credit card, except the card has been programmed with radio frequencies."

Palmer continued, "He swore up and down that if you placed this card underneath a glass of wine it would open the bouquet very quickly and the wine would taste much better than a glass of exactly the same wine without the card underneath. So we did a blind taste testing in front of different local sommeliers, and to our astonishment they kept choosing the wine that had been sitting on the card as the superior wine."

Palmer shrugged, well aware of how ridiculous his tale sounded. "I guess the moral of the story is you can't dismiss anyone out of hand; they may have a scheme or device that could make millions." Palmer subsequently arranged funding for radio-programmed wine sticks, which are used in some restaurants today.

Advancing the business schemes of other people either with money or sweat equity kept Palmer's enthusiasm at a level reminiscent of his pre-DDB days, and he became involved in everything from cosmetics to coffee companies. He also considered dabbling in online businesses from dating services to gambling. "I'm open to any kind of product and service, and invite anyone to pitch me, although you have to be careful doing business with people you know, because, while they may have the best intentions at heart, they don't necessarily have the business sense to succeed," he said. "And I won't put any equity into something I don't think will work. It's like the old saying: I have to believe in a product before I can lie about it."

But as usual, Palmer's more outrageous activities drew the most attention, such as posing nude for the cover of the trade magazine *Ad Pages* (thankfully, staged in a manner that concealed his privates), or one unforgettable incident in which, to celebrate a friend's birthday, he gleefully spent four hours in a makeup chair, selected the appropriate clothing and then strode through the DDB office as Francine Palmer. Older staff members politely looked away, and Palmer took the ruse to the next level by zeroing in on younger staff members and surreptitiously offering them sexual favours—all the while trying mightily to keep a straight face as sweat broke out on their brows.

When Palmer lured Lance Saunders away from a career with Leo Burnett Worldwide in Minneapolis and charged him with helping to run DDB's Canadian operations in 2010 (first in Vancouver, then in Toronto), Saunders's inauguration took the form of being the butt of a series of practical jokes. "It was school kid stuff and I should have known better, but I fell for every one of them because I didn't expect a man of Frank's stature to pull gags, especially such corny ones," he says.

The first occurred on the day Saunders was welcomed to the Vancouver office. Staff had presented him with a gift bag stuffed with local coffee, smoked salmon and other made-in-BC goods, and no sooner did they depart than Palmer urged Saunders to open it.

"I'd rather open it when I get back to my family," Saunders replied, the glow of being welcomed conflicting with a palpable sense of unease in undertaking the daunting task of gaining favour with DDB.

Maintaining his smile but his voice assuming a slightly harder tone, Palmer said, "Oh come on, open the damned thing, it's no big deal."

Not wanting to upset his benefactor, Saunders turned his back to Palmer and began opening the elaborately wrapped bag—which allowed Palmer to extract a glass vial from his jacket and crack it in half. Instantly, an intense smell of feces filled the room; as Saunders gagged and the odour billowed into the open-air Vancouver headquarters, a gleeful Palmer stood in the doorway and told dozens of grimacing staff members, "Look at this guy. He's so nervous about his new job that he just shit himself!"

Saunders recalls, "As everyone burst out laughing, I thought to myself, 'My God, is every day going to be like this?'"

Subsequently, Saunders's solitary late-night toil in his office was interrupted periodically by a ghostly whisper coming from what seemed to be the very air he was breathing. "I could have sworn the voice whispered, 'Did you hear me?'" he says. "I would dismiss it as my imagination—being alone at night and tired, that sort of thing—and get back to work, and then the voice would return.

"I got so freaked out that I called in one of the cleaning ladies and told her to stand there and listen. She stood silently for a few minutes and heard nothing, and several minutes after she left the whisper sounded again. I thought I was going mad."

Saunders soon learned that he had fallen for Palmer's all-time favourite gag, the Eviltron electronic device no bigger than a quarter that could be planted anywhere in a room and emitted strange sounds for months on end.

As a newcomer, Saunders was both impressed and appalled by the extent to which Palmer would reuse and refine his gags for different unsuspecting audiences. On one occasion, Palmer took Saunders for lunch at a nearby downtown sports bar, where a hockey playoff was being televised on flat screens to a boisterous, cheering crowd.

No sooner did they order than Palmer extracted a key fob-sized remote-control device from his pocket. Saunders recalls, "You've seen this thing before, and it's driven the DDB Vancouver receptionist crazy, but it was new to me. Just as a crucial moment in the game approached and the lunch patrons were holding their breaths waiting to see what would happen, Frank pressed a button, and all the flat screens shut off."

Struggling to maintain a straight face as a collective shout reverberated throughout the premises, Palmer watched as the bar manager dashed to a control panel to reactivate the televisions. The game reappeared on the screens, the crowd settled down and when it looked like the home team was about to score another goal, Palmer pressed the button and the screens went dark again.

This time the viewers leaped out of their chairs, swearing at the frazzled manager, who hurried over to the control panel and turned the power back on. Saunders says, "Sure as hell, several minutes later when the home team was manoeuvring into position for another win, Frank pressed the button, the screens went black and the lunch crowd went ballistic.

"Frank did this two more times until tears were running down his face and the crowd was at the point where I was sure they were about to break things. I pleaded with him, 'Frank, if they find out you're doing this, we'll be tarred and feathered or at the very least beaten up.' He eventually stopped, and I was in a cold sweat when we left the premises."

One stunt Palmer would prefer to forget wasn't of his own doing. Marika, who wished more than ever that her husband would at least consider semi-retirement but knew deep down it would never happen, helped reconcile herself to her fate by accepting a role as a recurring guest on the Slice cable network television reality show *The Real Housewives of Vancouver*; production of the show began in August 2011. "I'd just turned fifty-one and *Housewives* did great things for my self-esteem, although Frank was really apprehensive about me signing on," she says. "When the show's lawyers presented me with the legal documents for me to sign, he went over them with a fine-toothed comb. And then he said, 'Don't do it, it's a real piece-of-shit series.' But I signed anyway—and proceeded to have a blast."

The show aired in April 2012, and Marika was introduced in the second episode, "Oh, Bully!" in which she organizes a swank thirtieth birthday party at the Palmer condo for housewife Christina. As the series title suggests, *Housewives* is about the largely aimless antics of a group of rich Vancouver socialites, which has prompted critics to use terms such as "BOTOX fantasy" and "facelift odyssey" to describe the goings-on.

The hook for most of the forty-six-minute episode "Oh, Bully!" is that a particularly meddlesome housewife has been added to the party guest list, causing the other guests to worry that Christina may not show up for her own celebration.

Marika appears early in the episode driving a brand new cream Bentley, and later the action shifts to the Palmers' homestead high above downtown Vancouver as she prepares the party.

Palmer downplayed his opinion about *Housewives* whenever the series was mentioned in public, and to those who watched "Oh Bully!" his embarrassment was understandable: as the episode wound its way toward the climax of Christine's party, virtually every corner of the Palmers' condo was revealed in all of its opulence. Palmer himself was one of the party attendees, and at one point he was shown playfully falling onto a guest bed with one of the housewives as Marika looked on tolerantly. "I don't like rich people showing off what they've got, but that's exactly what *Housewives* did with that episode," he says.

Unfortunately for Palmer, *Housewives* was the highest-rated premiere in Slice's history, attracting 1.2 million viewers; subsequent episodes garnered 68 per cent higher ratings than the network had anticipated. To Palmer's chagrin, whenever he was interviewed on local television talk shows about developments in the ad world, he found himself fielding questions about *Housewives*. "I don't think I'll ever live it down," he said at one point.

The series didn't escape the attention of ON Positioning, a career management coaching company that Palmer had retained to assess his leadership performance. In a five-page, November 2012 assessment that ON Positioning founder Trevor Cape prepared, he sounds a single discordant note: "Appearing on *Real Housewives of Vancouver* contributed to the internal resentment that some feel about leaders' lavish lifestyle within an agency that appears to be scrimping and saving at every turn. But a big broadcast audience does suit his larger-than-life persona, and it would be good for him to find more ways to participate in the broadcast arena."

Alan Gee agrees. "Frank's a natural for television. I hope and expect he'll soon get a series of his own. If the Kardashians can do it, he certainly can, and he could show the world what the ad game is all about."

CHAPTER ELEVEN

Move On

A cruel truth of life is that the more it is lived, the quicker it passes. This is not lost on achievers such as Palmer, who carry on full tilt while oblivious to the passing years and are occasionally sobered by the weathered face staring back at them in the bathroom mirror.

Inevitably, those occasions are accompanied by brief moments of introspection: Am I as energetic as I was during my twenties? Do I have the same degree of curiosity?

Usually with achievers, the answers are yes and yes, and there is a wry humour in contemplating that one's intellectual acumen is at an all-time high—such a shame it had to come so late in life.

With the queasy knowledge that most of one's future dreams have become memories, the question becomes, What now? The only answer: stay clear, sharp and as fit as possible. Because the only acceptable end to this fleeting existence is dying while still contributing, rather than taking.

Life in all its terrifying beauty is not for the faint-hearted, and Frank Palmer doesn't so much realize this as it is embedded in the primal part of his brain.

Many people in the ad world assumed Palmer would eventually retire, despite his frequent claims that he would still be in the game at one hundred, and no doubt competitors looked forward to the day he would finally call it quits.

Certainly, at a time in Western society when a rigorous devotion to labour is associated with sickness (as anyone who has been accused of being a "workaholic" will attest), Palmer retiring would have been widely viewed as a just reward after so many decades of accomplishments—as if work itself has no intrinsic or celebratory worth.

But Palmer in his early seventies stubbornly maintained course, and because his workplace buzzed with people a lot younger than him, he was rarely reminded of how people his age were expected to behave.

But sometimes convention intruded. One weekend in 2013 he made the mistake of accepting an invitation to play golf with some friends, on the grounds he was a novice to the sport and curious about why it attracted so many enthusiasts. "Christ, what a waste of time that turned out to be," he told his assistant Veronica on Monday morning.

Suffering through nine holes of what Palmer considered to be a pointless game was irritating enough, but a worse fate awaited him in the changing room of the clubhouse. "Everyone stood around in their golf shirts and slacks saying things like, 'I whittled down my handicap another few points—what about you, Al?' and Al replies, 'Well, it was an improvement over last week.' 'Yeah, but last week was raining, so it wasn't your fault.' 'Yeah, I guess, but the week before wasn't so great either.'"

Palmer rose out of his chair and imitated his golf mates by slumping his shoulders and pushing his gut out. As Veronica burst out laughing, he hobbled about his office like an old man. "That's how they walked. They walked like they talked: old and slow. This is what life becomes for some people. I wanted to stick my head in an oven."

Plus, Palmer could more easily become the victim of practical jokes in surroundings as unfamiliar as a golf course. "When a bunch of office managers decided to hit the links during a trip to Palm Springs, I managed to switch Frank's ball with one that would explode on impact," Kevin Brady recalls. "Frank swung, the ball burst into an enormous white cloud of dust and he just stood there with his mouth open; he actually thought the sheer force of his swing had caused the ball to evaporate."

Amusingly, despite Palmer's aversion to golf, NABS West that year named its annual golf tournament in his honour for his unwavering contribution to charity. "He's no golfer, but the Palmer Invitational fundraiser is always a huge success," said Sue Belisle, chair of the annual NABS golf tournament. Palmer's involvement with the tournament began when he took over as sponsor of the event from *The Vancouver Sun/Province* newspapers and "put in way more money than he needed to," according to Belisle.

Far more energizing than Palmer's afternoon at the clubhouse was the youthful talent that surrounded him at the office. "Most of our people are in their thirties or younger, and what interests me is how smart they are, how up they are on things," he said. "They read a great deal and are keenly interested in furthering their careers. Better yet, they won't sit back and accept everything you say, which was pretty much the norm when I was their age. They challenge the hell out of you, and I enjoy that enormously."

Palmer has a funny effect on people: when a meeting with him is over, the sensation one has is akin to falling out of a moving automobile; you are suddenly inert and watching the car accelerate into the distance. Over time, Palmer will stay in touch via email (usually delivering a joke or cartoon), but the longer the separation, the more acute is the feeling that he is far down the road and you're still brushing off the dust in his wake—even if your life is as cluttered and hectic as his.

Palmer had promised his close friends that when he turned seventy-five, "there will be a big life change. I can't say what it is because I don't know what it will be. But I won't be doing the same thing I'm doing now. I might not even be with DDB. Who knows."

Those who didn't attend his seventy-fifth birthday and lost track of his daily activities wondered if a major life change had taken place. If he was an unlikely candidate for retirement, then surely he would slow down? After all, the body has a limited supply of energy.

It was therefore somewhat surprising for them to find Palmer in 2017, age seventy-seven, still maintaining course, still at DDB and often at his desk before sunrise, and often returning home late after a night of drinking in the finest bars of Vancouver (or Toronto, New York or Palm Springs).

His face and silky voice are unchanged, and so is his impatience. He still has the unnerving habit of walking soundlessly, startling people because he seems to materialize into rooms instead of enter them.

The only discernible change is a notable one: he is much less frustrated with DDB than he had been four years prior.

Around him, the technology that just four years before had been poised to fundamentally change the advertising world is now an inextricable part of everyday life. Many millennials now communicate entirely by text or email. In newsrooms, young reporters find it difficult to talk to people on the phone (once the lifeline of any journalist), let alone meet them in person. Smart phones are used to remotely control the lights and heating in one's home, or to check into a hotel and unlock the door to one's suite.

The flow of information is now not only relentless but it also pumps twenty-four hours a day through iPads, smart phones and even watches. The collective memory of doing things without being linked in is rapidly fading. So too, for many, is firsthand understanding of the physical world, which renders them especially fearful of events as innocuous as an unexpected snowfall or a particularly hot summer.

People born prior to the internet age are split into two camps: those who embrace the technology (such as Bob Stamnes and many other classic ad men) and those who are appalled by how it is changing human behaviour (a valid concern, considering how difficult it is for many millennials who spend hours staring at desktop and mobile screens instead of making eye contact with other people).

Since 2013, the internet and social media have made huge inroads in transforming advertising, as evidenced by Bob Stamnes's firm, Elevator. Not only did he relocate to a new building in East Vancouver amid a hub of advertising companies (including

Hootsuite), but also the layout of the building is radically different from his previous headquarters on Granville Island. Instead of offices and cubicles, everyone works in a single, huge room, which has a polished concrete floor and elegant furniture, and the room is divided by a communal kitchen, washrooms and a staircase.

Stamnes's "office" is located in one corner, and downstairs is space he shares in a partnership with creative talent unrelated to advertising (the only commonality being that they rely on the internet for disseminating ideas and doing business).

When Palmer visited Stamnes's new digs for the first time, his eyes twinkled. "Bobby, I love it," he said. "Maybe I could get an office for myself here."

In March of 2017 Stamnes took time out from his hectic schedule to explain what the "fundamental" change to advertising has been. "Experts and people like myself have talked endlessly about the impact of the internet and social media, but if, for example, we look at the shift between information in a newspaper and online, the only thing that's changed is the method with which information is disseminated. That's not a fundamental shift per se.

"On a social level, what has fundamentally changed is people's expectations and behaviour due to technology. For the advertising industry, the fundamental change is that technology has caused us to be enormously fragmented and chaotic—because the competition is no longer the company down the street or even the digital experts: the competition is the average guy living next door to you doing something from his basement. Unlike the mavericks of my generation or generations past, this person doesn't need much capital beyond securing a workplace."

Unlike professional photographers who panicked earlier in the new millennium when publishers began buying photos that average citizens had taken with their smart phones, Stamnes has considerable empathy for the basement dweller he just described. "Look, everybody is a frustrated ad man, and now technology has enabled them to be experts, and this is entirely logical. After all, everybody has seen way more ads than they've ever seen art or news or entertainment or anything else in their lives."

Stamnes, ever flamboyant in his love for colourful bow ties and unfailingly upbeat, adds, "The other fundamental shift is that companies that used to be clients can now easily, due to technology, take everything in-house. This is fine if you're a brand unto yourself such as Tom Ford, but it's dangerous for any other type of company because the objectivity that is essential to creative thinking is absent. In its place is the company boss coming up with an idea and all his staff nodding their heads and telling him how great that idea is. I mean, fuck off!"

It's worth noting that the rapidity of fundamental change in the ad industry is such that it made the work setting of Hootsuite, widely viewed as revolutionary in 2013, seem cosmetic. Back then, Palmer's biographer was given a tour through Hootsuite's cavernous, open-space Vancouver headquarters, where creative staff were slumped in beanbag sofas, typing out copy on their iPads; the conference room was a tent with wood park benches in the middle of rows of workstations; dogs belonging to other staffers roamed freely; yoga rooms, nap rooms (complete with army cots), a gym and a gaming area were well attended, all in the name of fostering inspiration.

In the face of the fundamental transformation that would soon come, Hootsuite's radical approach to conducting business now seems hopelessly outdated.

Continuing his discourse, Stamnes addresses those in his industry who feel uncomfortable that the "good old days" are over. "With the greatest of respect to them, they must take some responsibility for the demise, at least with regard to consolidations and mergers. And it's worth pointing out that for every big consolidated agency, there's someone with skin in the game. There's not much moving of the deck chairs anymore, but a growing number of clients are using different agencies for different things."

He concludes, "What will never change in our business is the idea. Ideas are the fundamentals; it's only that they exist now in a state of tumult. But that tumult also represents incredible promise and opportunity. The trick is to find the best and most profitable ways to funnel these ideas, and we're all engaged in this process."

For his part, Palmer sees tumult for the ad industry in the years ahead, and he too doesn't necessarily think this is a bad thing. "The biggest change or opportunity will happen as new communication models are created," he says. "This, in my opinion, will not come from the large or current advertising agency models that exist today. Internet companies like Google, Apple and Facebook, and gaming companies, are creating new opportunities.

"These companies will steal all the agencies' clients in a few short years. The saving grace for the agency business is to find a new and better way to get paid, and it will not be for hours spent. It will be for value creation, and payment will be based on results. Agencies must find ways to get paid royalties and licensing fees; they must also build a positive reputation for their clients. This can happen only by creating valuable, engaging content that's targeted to the intended customer."

At seventy-eight, Palmer is unique in that he has brought all of his twentieth-century trappings into the strange and daunting twenty-first century—and they are as readily embraced by younger colleagues as their technology is embraced by him. Does this suggest some of his old-fashioned values might eventually rub off on the younger crowd? "If you mean Frank's devotion to face-to-face relationships and communications, it would be great to think so," says Stamnes.

Palmer's admiration for youth is a big reason why he is much less frustrated by DDB in 2017 compared to four years prior. "Wonderful new people are steering the ship," he says. "Wendy Clark, the CEO of DDB Worldwide, is an incredible talent and a breath of fresh air for the company, as are Kevin Brady, Lance Saunders and Steve Carli—all presidents and CEOs of their divisions.

"These people are the collective new face of DDB, and they make me feel much brighter about the future."

It follows, then, that Palmer supports youthful ambition whenever he has the opportunity. One recent example that particularly impressed NABS West's Sue Belisle occurred in 2016, when Palmer learned that the purse for the winner of the pro-am league (in which talented amateur golfers tee off with tour players) was only $600. "He hated the idea of someone trying to reach the professional leagues being awarded that sum, so he dipped into his pocket and made it an even $10,000," she says.

At DDB, Palmer views his function with mixed feelings. "I guess I'm Yoda. My job is to travel back and forth between different offices and make sure everything is running smoothly. I'm the guy in the control tower making sure the airplanes are taking off and landing safely, and as a result I make a shitload of money for the company."

Even though the corporate makeup has evolved to the point where Palmer knows he could leave DDB Canada in good hands, it's pointless to ponder something that will never happen. "You asked if I've changed in four years, and I don't mean to sound like a broken record, but aside from looking older I honestly don't feel any different from when I turned forty," he says.

Not even being a grandfather to two girls, eight and six, burdens him with the sensation of time running out. "Honestly, no. They're cute kids. It's fun watching them play, and I enjoy playing with them.

"As for my morning routine, I wake up around 5:00 AM fully refreshed and my mind going at a hundred miles an hour, even if I've been out drinking the night before. In fact, this morning I got up at 4:30 and began sending out emails—then I went back to bed because I realized I might be bugging people."

Does Palmer relish his role as the elder statesman of advertising passing his knowledge on to young talent? "No," he replies casually. "I'm sometimes referred to as 'The Man,' so there's a reputation out there. But a lot of it is myth. If you stick around long enough, you end up getting a lot of credit for things you didn't do. I don't really like admitting this, but I'm not that good. I'm capable of outlasting people, and at the end of the day maybe that's my greatest strength.

"That said, I'd still much rather be owner of a hockey team than the coach."

"Why?" his biographer asks.

Palmer, who is standing in the foyer of his Palm Springs home, which is a ten-minute drive from Frank Sinatra's estate, thinks the answer by now is obvious. "Because I would have complete control of everything. But what can you do? Quit, I guess. I obviously haven't quit, because I love the business too much and I'm still having too much fun, and I also realized something about myself four years ago."

"What?"

"I realized I was focusing so much on my frustrations that I was getting myself into a worse state than necessary, and it bothered me that I could become someone that nobody wanted to be around. There's nothing like a complainer to sap the life out of any party, so I focused instead on the terrific money I'm making, the great life I have and the fact that I'll still be the same when I'm one hundred."

As if to underscore that his essential nature will never change, he suddenly shifts gears. "So, when's my biography going to be published?"

It's become a familiar out-of-left-field question, driven not by the notion that his story is over but by the urge to bring a project to conclusion. When he's reminded again of the date, he mutters something about creative work overall taking too much time to complete—then he launches into a pithy observation of a mutual long-time colleague who is in his sixties: "I bumped into him on the street the other day and almost knocked him over: fucking guy is looking pretty old these days."

Dean Mailey was once asked if he thinks his old friend is happy with his life so far, and after careful thought he replied, "I've wondered about that often, and the answer I've come up with is that Frank compartmentalizes. He looks at his career, and he's happy with it. He looks at his kids, and after some long struggles, he's happy with them. Other aspects of his life drive him crazy."

In other words, happiness—and life—for Frank is a series of individual moments that he chooses to focus on, much in keeping with his habit of beginning a conversation about one topic and in the very next sentence addressing something entirely different. "And then you factor in Frank constantly looking ahead rather than lamenting about the good old days," says Lance Saunders. "Yes, he loves telling stories about the good old days, but he has no interest in wishing for their return, because there's too much ahead of him. This makes him unusual, especially for his age."

Still waiting impatiently for his biography to be finished, Palmer dismisses the question of what inspires him to work harder by telling a joke. "A husband and wife visit a bull pen," he says. "The owner of the bulls points to one bull in a pen and says, 'He mated 150 times this year,' and the wife is obviously impressed by this. The couple move to another pen and are told that the bull in it mated 200 times—and the wife is even more impressed.

"They finally come face to face with a bull that has mated 365 times, and when the wife digs her husband in the ribs and informs him that's once a day, the husband replies, 'Yeah, but I'll bet it wasn't with the same cow!'"

Hugh Ruthven once remarked, "It is regrettable that Frank, a man of several talents, most notably painting, has never been able to take the giant leap and devote himself fully to something other than advertising. I often wonder what kind of a splash he would make in the art world if the circumstances were different."

Sensing this, Saunders of late has been coaxing Palmer to spend more time painting (a logical suggestion, considering Palmer spends as much time as he is legally allowed in his Palm Springs home conducting business). "And he seems to be responding," he says.

In March of 2017 Palmer proudly states, "I've painted half a dozen canvasses this year so far, all acrylic, all of them a western theme."

His work is strikingly minimalist, alive with primary colours, and it's tempting to imagine Palmer standing in a sun-filled room smeared with paint and stabbing a canvas with his brush, considering every stroke with a raised eyebrow, totally lost in the artistic process.

But although his skill is not in question, his latest wave of productivity is driven by a specific and familiar goal. He explains, "A gallery owner in Palm Springs who wants to exhibit the paintings keeps saying I could get $5,000 apiece for them, but I think I can get much more than that without too much effort."

Several years prior, Palmer had painted a rendering of the iconic Il Giardino restaurant for owner Umberto Menghi, who was closing his establishment in order to focus on other business endeavours. "I made 250 copies of that rendering, and the prints were identical to the original," he recalls. "I sold each one and donated the proceeds to the Vancouver Police Foundation, and if I could do that with my own paintings, subtly adjusting each print and adding highlights, I could sell multiple copies—say, ten for $25,000."

What's noteworthy is that even though a gallery owner has deemed Palmer's art worthy of exhibition in the United States (something any true artist would kill for), Palmer is more excited by the prospect of commercializing his efforts and maximizing profits. "Why not?" he argues. "Once a painting is done, it's dead to me. On to the next one."

As 2017 unfolds, Stamnes anticipates that Palmer will soon deliberately place himself in a situation—could be business, could be personal—that will take considerable energy and skill to resolve. "At the end of the day, he's driven by fear, and he puts himself on the edge to sustain that fear. In the old days this would take the form of perhaps him buying a house that he couldn't afford. Today the stakes will be much higher, and I look forward to seeing what he'll do next, because his constant state of edginess keeps him young, and it makes people like me, who used to believe that by the time you're in your late fifties your best years are behind you, realize that the best is only beginning."

Red Robinson, now eighty and still a popular DJ, agrees. "Risk today is a four-letter word. All people want is comfort and security, but those luxuries come at a huge price. Plus, comfort is fleeting, and you're never really as secure as you think. The fact is that risk built our industry. It built Canada, and it certainly made Frank what he is today. So whatever he plans for the future, it will probably involve a great deal of risk taking on his part. He doesn't know how to operate otherwise."

Palmer these days seizes every opportunity to keep things edgy, and everyone is fair game. Recently, the devil that is never far from the surface compelled him to focus on Marika's fondness for Belvedere Vodka, branded as the world's first luxury vodka. Convinced that clever marketing, and not the quality of what is essentially a flavourless spirit, has attracted connoisseurs in droves to the beverage, he waited until his wife finished a bottle, retrieved it from the kitchen garbage and walked to the nearest liquor store.

There, he purchased the cheapest rotgut vodka available, poured it into the Belvedere bottle, carefully resealed it, went home and placed the bottle on the kitchen counter. Marika, thinking he'd purchased it for her as a gift, gratefully poured herself a drink, sat back and sipped contentedly.

A week or so later, when the bottle was empty, Palmer asked, "So, how did you like your vodka?"

"It was delicious—I love Belvedere," came the reply.

Palmer triumphantly delivered the bad news, and all he will say two weeks later of the response is, "She's still pissed at me!"

And now he decides to focus yet again on his biography, as well as on the biographer, who confesses to being unsure of the best way to finish the story. "Why are you trying to turn something easy into something that's difficult?" Palmer shouts at one point.

"I'm not—it would just be good if this could end on a profound note."

"Oh, for Christ's sake," he replies.

Palmer gets up from his chair, framed by the windows and rooftops of downtown Vancouver beyond his office. It's 9 AM; the clouds have cleared and the sun is shining, and through his walls one can hear the laughter and calling of DDB staff.

"Look," Palmer says. "Forget profundities. All you need to do is wind everything down, tack 'The End' onto it and move on to something else. That's what you have to do with everything."

THE END

Acknowledgements

Anna Comfort O'Keeffe, Jesmine Cham and Sarah Weber: I am in your debt. A writer couldn't ask for better editors!

To my publishers: Thank you sincerely, first for Red, and now for Frank.

And special thanks to Frank Palmer, who showed me you can be thirty-nine forever.